Supporting Research Students

Barbara Allan

facet publishing

© Barbara Allan 2010

Published by Facet Publishing
7 Ridgmount Street, London WC1E 7AE
www.facetpublishing.co.uk

Facet Publishing is wholly owned by CILIP: the Chartered Institute of
Library and Information Professionals.

British Library Cataloguing in Publication Data
A catalogue record for this book is available from the British Library.

ISBN 978-1-85604-685-5

First published 2010

Text printed on FSC accredited material.

Mixed Sources
Product group from well-managed
forests and other controlled sources
www.fsc.org Cert no. SA-COC-1565
© 1996 Forest Stewardship Council

Typeset from author's files in 10/15 pt Century Schoolbook and
Franklin Gothic by Facet Publishing.
Printed and made in Great Britain by MPG Books Group, UK.

Contents

List of figures

List of tables

Acknowledgements

Thank you to the many people in the library and information profession who have shared ideas, answered queries and discussed their experiences of supporting research students with me. Particular thanks must go to the participants, representing a diverse range of universities and research institutions, in my 'Supporting research students' workshops at CILIP as their experiences and questions have shaped this book.

Thank you to Rowena Macrae-Gibson, Liaison Librarian, London School of Economics Library, and Dr Jane Secker, Learning Technology Librarian, Centre for Learning Technology, London School of Economics, for providing the case study 'MI512 Research training course for PhD students', which is presented in Chapter 6.

Many thanks to Dr Cecilia Loureiro-Koechlin and Dr Chris Thomson, whose work on the Hull University Business School Virtual Graduate School, and the Graduate Virtual Research Environment respectively helped to inform Chapter 7. In addition, both Cecilia and Chris have answered my queries and helped me to keep up to date on a range of technical matters.

Thank you to Professor Jerry Wellington of the School of Education at the University of Sheffield for his support during my doctoral studies. He has influenced my ways of thinking about research. Many thanks to my friend and colleague Sheena Banks, of the School of Education at the University of Sheffield – our conversations about research, supporting research students and virtual graduate schools have had a major impact on my thinking and on this book.

I would like to thank colleagues at the University of Hull, in particular in the Business School, who have supported my endeavours in this field. Finally, thank you to Denis and Sarah for providing me with their constant support during this project.

Barbara Allan

1

Introduction

This chapter provides an introduction to this book and also to the world of research and research students. The book is written as a general guide and I suggest that you read this chapter and then skim through the rest of the book. You may then choose when to read individual chapters in depth. They are designed to be read and worked through in any order.

The aim of this book is to provide library and information workers in the higher education sector with an understanding of the research process and to help them support research students. Library and information workers in higher education institutions are likely to provide well established support services for undergraduate and postgraduate students on taught programmes. In contrast, support services for research students are often not so well established as those that are focused on students on taught programmes, and in some cases may be relatively novel, e.g. as a result of some higher education institutions developing and expanding their research student base. The support needs of research students have recently risen up the academic agenda and this is linked to a number of factors.

The traditional taught doctorate, the PhD, has been joined by a range of doctoral qualifications including the 'professional' doctorate such as the Doctor in Business Administration (DBA), the Doctorate in Education (EdD) and psychology (DClinPsy or DEdPsy), and this diversification has led to a more diverse student body, which now includes senior professional practitioners. Chiang (2003) identified that the learning needs of doctoral research students have undergone rapid change and development. He observed that doctoral education has shifted its focus from an experience enabling entry into an academic community and career, to a qualification for entry into the wider labour market. This puts emphasis on doctoral students gaining a wider set of employability skills. The issue of employability skills is explored in Chapter 5.

While the library and information profession is a graduate one, with many individuals having a taught Master's degree, a relatively small number of workers have a research degree. This means that most will not have experienced and internalized the distinct learning processes involved in achieving a doctorate. This book provides guidance on the research process and on research degrees, and it outlines the ways in which library and information workers can support the specialist needs of these students.

My motivation for writing this book came as a result of my experiences as a part-time research student working towards a Doctorate in Education in a UK university. This was an extremely positive experience, and discussions with my fellow students during residential weekend schools led me to appreciate both the diversity of this group of students and their greatly differing previous educational backgrounds and experiences. My student cohort included international and home students; all of us worked in education, ranging from primary to higher education, with some in specialist areas, e.g. speech therapy or special education. Those of us who worked in higher education were familiar with the support structures and the resources available to us. This sometimes meant that we used the library and information resources of our employing university rather than of the one where we had enrolled as students. In contrast, other students had more than 30 years' professional work experience since studying for their first degree and had little experience of modern academic libraries. They soon appreciated the massive changes in the information landscape and the importance of digital resources. Some students had access to administrative support, including researchers who would carry out initial literature searches for them. Most of us had to rely on our own information skills and develop them by engaging with the range of learning opportunities offered by the university's library and information staff.

My research for this book involved the following activities:

■ a literature search
■ discussions with current doctorate students and their supervisors
■ discussions with graduates who had successfully completed their doctorates
■ discussions with library and information professionals who attended my workshops 'Supporting research students' held at the Chartered Institution of Library and Information Professionals (CILIP)
■ discussions with colleagues at the University of Hull and the University of Sheffield who were involved in the development of virtual graduate schools.

Structure of this book

This chapter provides an introduction to the book and also to the world of research and research students. This includes a brief overview of different types of doctorates. It concludes with a brief discussion about supporting research students.

The subject of research and the research process is vast, and, in Chapter 2, I provide an introduction to the main milestones and the terminology used in the field. The aim of the chapter is to provide library and information workers with a general understanding of research and its language. It considers different styles of research, from positivist to interpretivist research, and also different research methods. Due to the vast scope of the subject, I have selected common research approaches, and methods, and so this is an indicative rather than an exhaustive introduction to research.

In Chapters 3 and 4, I consider the research process as experienced by a research student. Although every research student's experience is unique, in these chapters I attempt to provide an overview of the research journey and discuss typical milestones such as the research proposal, upgrade seminar, writing up and the viva (oral examination). In Chapter 3, I outline the role of the academic supervisor and also explore the initial experiences of a research student from application to university through to the design of the research process. I cover topics such as induction, working with a supervisor and getting started. Chapter 4 provides an overview of the research process, which begins with the acceptance of the research proposal and continues through to completion and obtaining a doctorate. The chapter covers topics such as the literature review, methodology, fieldwork, writing up, the *viva voce* examination, amendments and completing the doctorate.

Research students need a range of skills to enable them to successfully complete their individual research and obtain a doctorate. These include information skills. In addition, they need to develop a range of skills that will enable them to obtain employment, whether as academics, researchers or within a particular profession. Research students, particularly those taking part in a professional doctorate, may also need to develop their employability skills, e.g. to enable them to move from a management to a strategic role. Chapter 5 considers the skills required by research students and, in particular, information skills.

Many academic library and information workers are involved in supporting research students, and this is the focus of Chapter 6. The chapter explores different approaches to supporting research students, including induction, workshops, one-to-one support and electronic support. Approaches for targeting and communicating with research students are also considered here.

Chapter 7 considers the rise of the virtual graduate school. The concept for the virtual graduate school is an online environment where research students can come together to access a range of resources, and also to meet and discuss common issues with each other and, perhaps, with their supervisors. Two different approaches to developing a virtual graduate school are explored in some depth in this chapter.

An important aspect of becoming a researcher and completing a doctorate is joining a research community. Many doctoral students embark on a journey in their doctoral process which enables them to engage in a specialist research community that is often global in nature. These communities frequently cluster around a small number of international experts and come together at conferences and communicate with each other via electronic means. Chapter 8 provides an introduction to research communities in the context of supporting doctoral students.

Finally, Chapter 9 considers professional development for library and information workers in the support of research students. Different approaches to professional development are considered, and these include support offered by professional organizations and networks, provision offered by higher education institutions, and the role of research degrees.

Introduction to the world of research and research students

Research and knowledge creation are a central part of university life. Individual researchers and also research teams engage in systematic investigations using research approaches and methods relevant to their specific discipline. These activities may be funded by external bodies, such as the research councils or large organizations, or they may be funded by the university. The outputs of research are disseminated via conference papers (to academic peers) and research reports (aimed at funding bodies), and much research will be published in peer reviewed journals. These initial outputs are often written in an academic and very technical language, which makes them not readily accessible to a wider audience. A wider form of dissemination may occur through articles in the professional , as well as through monographs and textbooks.

Following the above summary, the world of research will now be explored in some more detail, starting with researchers, who may be students carrying out a research degree and working under the supervision of an experienced researcher. Researchers also include individuals who have completed their doctoral degrees and have obtained research posts (often referred to as 'post-docs'); people who are employed on temporary research posts which may be funded by external grants; and academic staff, including lecturers, senior or principal lecturers, readers and professors. There is a very large group of contract research staff in the UK. Academic staff are likely to be performing their research activities as part of their workload, which will include teaching and academic administration duties. Research teams are likely to be led by a senior academic, often a professor, and teams may vary in size from one or two members up to 12 or 16.

Research activities are often funded by external organizations, and in the UK the main bodies include the research councils:

- Arts and Humanities Research Council (AHRC)
- Biotechnology and Biological Sciences Research Council (BBSRC)
- Engineering and Physical Science Research Council (EPSRC)
- Economic and Social Research Council (ESRC)
- Medical Research Council (MRC)
- Natural Environment Research Council (NERC).

In addition, funding is available from a range of bodies, including:

- the Association of Medical Research Charities
- the Leverhulme Trust
- the Wellcome Trust.

Private companies and voluntary organizations also fund research.

Competition for funds is extremely strong and the bidding process involves producing a research proposal that includes evidence that the research ideas are located within the literature of the discipline and that the research activity will lead to the creation of new knowledge. Research teams are likely to work intensively on producing a high quality bid to a strict deadline, and this frequently means late-night working without any assurance that the bid will be successful. Bids need to demonstrate excellence or innovation, and they need to be written so that they meet the aims and objectives of the funding body. The selection process is based on peer review. If the bid is successful, then the principal investigator (the director of the research project) will have to draw together a research team and lead the project so that it meets the research outcomes.

Research teams produce a variety of outputs, including:

- conference papers (which may or may not be peer reviewed)
- reports aimed at the funding organization or other stakeholders in the research process
- academic journal articles in peer reviewed journals
- articles in the professional literature and high quality newspapers
- presentations at professional conferences
- press releases for academic and funding body websites.

In addition, as the new knowledge becomes accepted within its discipline, it may be included in a student textbook or a monograph written by a specialist in that field.

The concept of 'peer review' is important in the world of academic research. Academic journal articles and also bids for funds are commonly reviewed by other academics who are experts in the field, and the process is normally anonymous. This means that in order for an article to be published or for a bid to be approved for funding, it must be reviewed and approved by other academics in the same field.

This helps to maintain the quality and integrity of the research process.

The production and dissemination of knowledge

This section outlines the processes involved in both creating and disseminating knowledge. One of the main functions of universities is to create and disseminate new knowledge through research. Academics are likely to be involved in research activities as well as their teaching activities. Many lecturers work in research teams with colleagues from their own university, research institutions or from higher education institutions from around the world. Sometimes these teams will include doctoral students working on their theses. The research may be funded by the university, a government body, a private company or a sponsor.

Figure 1.1 shows some of the characteristics of a typical research process. Teams will normally carry out research, write up and then discuss their initial findings with colleagues. This often happens at conferences where an individual or a small team presents their findings for discussion and debate among members of the research community interested in that particular topic or theme. This communication with peers is an important characteristic of the research process and helps to ensure that the research meets the high standards required by the international research community. Once a research team has obtained feedback on its initial findings or ideas, it will perhaps carry out more research and/or edit and amend its work to take on board the feedback. Finally, the research will be submitted for publication, e.g. as a formal report for the funder or as an article in an academic journal.

Journal articles are normally peer reviewed before they are published. The journal editor sends the article to academic experts in the particular field who will assess it and ensure that the researcher/team has produced a high quality piece of research. They will check the research methods and the knowledge claims in the

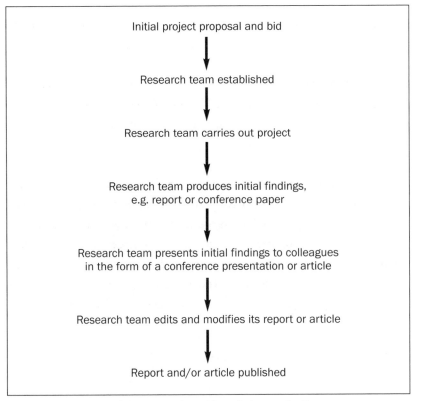

Initial project proposal and bid

Research team established

Research team carries out project

Research team produces initial findings,
e.g. report or conference paper

Research team presents initial findings to colleagues
in the form of a conference presentation or article

Research team edits and modifies its report or article

Report and/or article published

Figure 1.1 *Overview of the research and knowledge production process*

article. Once the editor is satisfied by the peer review process that the article is well written and makes an original contribution to knowledge in the specific field, it will be accepted for publication. This process enables knowledge developed as part of the research process to be disseminated to the wider academic community and ensures that journal articles are of a high quality. It also highlights the importance of journal articles as a means of disseminating original research and new ideas.

The last stage in the knowledge dissemination process occurs when the new knowledge is summarized and presented in forms that are likely to be used by practitioners. Academic writing in journal articles is often rather abstract and difficult to read. Consequently, the main findings that are reported in such articles are often rewritten in a more accessible manner and printed as:

- articles in professional magazines, e.g. *Personnel Today, The Economist, Accountancy Age, Nursing Today*
- articles in good quality newspapers, e.g. the *Financial Times*
- summaries in textbooks.

The knowledge process is summarized in Figure 1.2. It is interesting to note that although a relatively small number of people may read the original academic article, large numbers may read a simplified version in types of publication such as those listed above. Research students are expected to read the original academic articles, though they may find that textbooks and summaries in the professional press provide a useful overview to the subject (see Chapter 5).

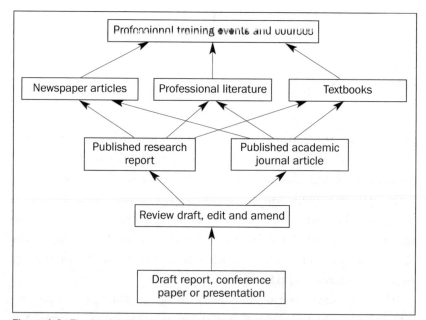

Figure 1.2 *The knowledge dissemination process*

Types of research degree

Research students are not a homogeneous group. Indeed, they are extremely diverse and will include full- and part-time students, students working as part of a research team or independently, and students based on campus and those who are researching from a distance. There are many different kinds of research degree.

The purpose of this section is to provide a rough guide to the different types of research degree. If you are reading this section and relating my overview to your own experiences in your own higher education institution, then my advice is to find out more about how research degrees are organized within your institution.

The traditional PhD involves independent research that is supervised by an academic supervisor and it is examined on the basis of a written thesis of typically 80,000 words and a *viva voce* (oral) examination. In the UK the length of study is typically three years full time, and students commonly take up to an additional year to write up and present their findings. It is now common for PhD students to take a series of taught modules in the first year or two of their studies. These modules, which provide credit towards the PhD, often focus on research methods and on specific research tools that the student will require later in their studies. In some universities students will be registered first for a Master in Research (MRes) or Master in Philosophy (MPhil), and once their progress towards the PhD has been assured, e.g. by an upgrading seminar or paper, then they are permitted to proceed to the doctorate. MPhil degrees may be awarded following a period of research rather than a course of study. In contrast, the MRes degree is a one-year full-time course that enables students to develop their knowledge and skills in research practices. While the MRes is sometimes used as the starting point for a PhD, another approach to the PhD is by publication, and this route is commonly taken by academics who have produced a series of quality academic papers, and possibly books. They may be asked to provide a paper that summarizes their research and its contribution to their field, and they may also be asked to attend a *viva voce* examination.

Professional and practice doctorates

Professional doctorates, such as the EdD (Doctorate in Education), DBA (Doctorate in Business Administration) or DInfSc (Doctorate in Information Science) were designed to enable practitioners in the workplace to obtain a doctorate through a series of taught modules and a thesis. As with the taught element of other programmes, these modules must be passed and they provide credit towards the degree. The thesis is an individual piece of research which is typically about 50,000 words long and likely to be work based.

My experience of gaining a professional doctorate in education through part-time study is fairly typical, as it involved two stages. Stage 1 was the taught element and I attended six residential weekends over a two-year period. Each weekend focused on a theme and the accompanying assessment activity was to write a 6000-word essay on a topic relevant to the theme and my own professional practice. Stage 2 involved another two-year period during which we worked individually on our research projects and the six residential weekends provided an opportunity for sharing of knowledge and experiences, supervision sessions and library work. I then took almost a year to write up my thesis and present it as a bound document and in the oral examination.

The advantages of studying for a professional doctorate include: the possibility of carrying out research and gaining a doctorate while still in full-time employment; the structured nature of the programme, i.e. two years' taught element and two years' individual research; and the benefits of working as part of a supportive professional network of like-minded individuals. The challenges include the difficulties of balancing work, home and research activities. Also, some people consider the traditional PhD as the 'only' quality route to gaining a doctorate.

Another form of research degree is the practice-based doctorate and this may include a variety of outputs, including a novel (for creative writing), a portfolio of work (for art and design) or performance pieces (for drama, theatre studies or music). These may be accompanied by a written element which includes a description of the context and critique of or reflection on the work(s). Examination may be on the basis of the written elements or performance, as well as an oral examination.

Readers are advised to find out about the different doctoral programmes offered by their higher education institutions and to obtain general information about them. This will help to provide a starting point for supporting research students.

Stakeholders in research degrees

Park (2007) identifies the stakeholders in research degrees as the students and their supervisors, academic departments and institutions, the actual disciplines, funding bodies and employers, and the nation as a whole. The key stakeholders are the students, who are likely to invest many years of their lives in working towards their doctorate. For many students, this involves leaving their home country and living and studying abroad. It may involve a house move for their family, and, for all research students, family and friends are frequently valuable supporters of the research endeavour. Students' motivations for gaining a doctorate will vary, and may include love of their subject, gaining an internationally recognized qualification, gaining the 'top' qualification in the world of universities, or gaining the qualification required for an academic career. For many students, their motivations may well be a mixture of reasons.

Academic supervisors choose to be involved in the supervision process for a number of different reasons, including the pleasure of facilitating a student's research and entry into academic life. This is rather like supporting an apprentice. Research supervisors may also co-author publications with their students, so enhancing their own publication records. The experience of supervision is also a valuable addition to an academic's *curriculum vitae*.

University departments welcome doctoral students, as they help to demonstrate that their departments are active in research, and they also provide a valuable income. Doctoral students also contribute to research centres and add to the academic life of departments. Many such research students are also involved in learning and teaching activities, e.g. holding seminars and tutorials, and running laboratory-based sessions or workshops. Individual universities and departments will have their own policies about the role doctoral students may take in their learning and teaching activities. At an institutional level, doctoral students help to provide credibility to the university's research agenda, and having research-degree-awarding powers is an indicator of the status and academic credibility of a university (Stauffer, 1990).

Research students work within the context of a discipline, and students often experience entry to the discipline and an academic career through the doctoral process as a crucial part of their doctorate is knowledge creation. This means that they help to maintain the discipline as they join its ranks and they also add to the intellectual life of the discipline through their own intellectual endeavours. In addition, they become the university researchers and academics of the future.

In the UK some research students are funded by bodies such as the Higher Education Funding Council for England (HEFCE) or the Research Councils. These bodies' support for research students and doctoral programmes helps to sustain the universities of the future by raising up new researchers and academics. In addition, the work of these students helps to create a critical mass in research teams (Park, 2007) and to ensure that there is a sustained output of high quality research that contributes both to university endeavours and to society.

Doctoral graduates have high-level skills that are valued by employers who want employees who offer critical thinking, systematic research skills and the ability to deal with complex subjects. In some countries and sectors a doctoral qualification is a prerequisite for certain types of employment, e.g. in research institutions, in the scientific and medical fields, and in the world of higher education. Finally, the production of doctoral graduates with high-level skills contributes to the nation's workforce and help to drive the knowledge economy.

Contemporary issues regarding supporting research students

As mentioned earlier, research students are not a homogeneous group of students. They are an extremely diverse group and will include full and part time students, students who work as part of a research team or independently, students who are based on-campus and those who are researching at a distance. They may range in age from their early 20s to their 90s, may be in full- or part-time employment, and may have families and caring responsibilities. Their financial positions will vary, with some students receiving generous sponsorship while others are self-financed. In addition, their previous educational experience will vary, ranging from students who have recently completed an undergraduate degree and have up-to-date skills in handling a wide range of information resources, to those who may not have any experience of using a modern library.

International students make up a significant part of the doctoral student body and, again, their previous educational experience and range of information skills may vary. Some may not have used a modern library with open access to resources; they may not be familiar with classification schemes such as the Dewey Decimal System and may have no experience of using journals (printed or electronic). In contrast, other international students will have high-level information skills and high expectations in terms of library and information resources.

Many research students will not have made extensive use of electronic journals, specialist tools such as citation indexes or interlibrary loans during their undergraduate degrees. Indeed, they may not be aware of the existence of these tools and resources. In contrast, some research students will have up-to-date knowledge of such information tools and will be highly skilled in carrying out advanced searches.

The extremely diverse nature of research students provides a challenge for library and information workers who support them. In many respects, supporting research students is much more challenging than supporting students on taught programmes, e.g. undergraduate students, where there is likely to be more common ground in terms of information skills. Practical approaches to supporting research students are considered in Chapter 6.

Summary

In this chapter, I have provided an introduction to the book, including a brief outline of the contents of each chapter. This was followed by an introduction to the world of research and research students. I provided a summary of the research process and of the subsequent knowledge dissemination and publication process. Then followed an overview of different types of doctorates, including the traditional PhD, the professional doctorate and the practice doctorate. Readers are advised to find out more about the research degrees offered by their institutions. The chapter concluded with a brief discussion of the diversity of research students and the implications for library and information workers

2

Research and the research process

Introduction

In this chapter, I provide an introduction to research and the research process. The aim is to provide library and information workers with a general understanding of research and the language of research. The chapter considers different styles of research, from positivist to interpretivist, and I consider different research methods.

The subject of research and the research process is vast, and academic libraries provide access to hundreds of textbooks on the subject. This makes providing an overview in a single chapter quite a challenge. Consequently, I have selected key ideas and themes and have attempted to indicate the overall shape of the research process and key terms related to it, rather than an exhaustive exposition of the subject. This account is thus very much a generalization and over-simplification. Each topic considered is in itself the focus of a number of textbooks and many research articles. If you require further information or want to explore the debates relating to individual research approaches and methods, then my advice is that you follow up the topic in the context of the discipline(s) that you support within your normal work roles.

Research proposal

The starting point for many research projects is a proposal, which a researcher may write either as a means of gaining funding from an external organization or as a means of gaining resources and permission to proceed from their own organization. A proposal is a written document that outlines what the researcher(s) intend to do in their project. Typically, proposals will be between 1000 and 2000 words long, although proposals in the form of funding bids may be even longer. Many organizations provide a template for producing the proposal or bid, and typical headings for its organization are likely to include:

- Title
- Introduction containing:
  - project aims and objectives, or research aims and hypotheses/questions
  - problem or issue to be addressed
  - context of the work, e.g. specific company or sector
  - scope of the work, e.g. what will be included and what will be excluded
  - unique features of the proposed research, e.g. innovation.
- Relevant literature. This will indicate the literature base for the work and seminal works. This section may be used to justify the proposed research, e.g. it may identify a gap in the literature. It may also be used to explore the proposed research methods and also to highlight potential problems that other researchers have experienced in this field.
- Context of the study. This section may be included in research in the social sciences, e.g. education, business and management, and will summarize the context of the study, such as an organization, business or school, or the relevant business sector, e.g. healthcare products, logistics and supply chain management. Desk-based research or scientific research which is not linked to a particular organization will not necessarily include this section.

■ Proposed methodology. This section will present the research approach, methodology and methods, including data collection and data analysis methods. It will also consider issues of access and ethics. It is likely that this section will be informed by the literature research and that the proposed methodology will be in alignment with common practice in the field of study. These topics are covered in the next section.

■ Issues of ethics and access. The proposal may identify how ethical issues will be dealt with throughout the research process.

■ Action plan. This will provide a detailed time schedule for the research.

■ Resource requirements, e.g. special resources that will be needed in order to carry out the research. These may vary from hundreds of pounds for very small and local research projects to millions for large-scale projects.

■ Researchers. This section will identify the lead researcher who is often called the principal investigator or PI, as well as the research team. It may include brief biographies of all team members.

■ Research outcomes. This section will describe the anticipated research outcomes.

■ Dissemination. This section will identify the methods that will be used to disseminate the research findings, e.g. conferences, journal articles, websites etc.

■ Initial list of references.

The production of a research proposal requires the researcher to have a good understanding of the research approach or paradigm, the research methodology and methods. These topics are described in the next section.

Research approach and methods

There is a vast literature on research and research methodologies, and each discipline has its own approach. The purpose of this section is to provide a general overview of common approaches and you are advised to refer to additional research methods textbooks if you require detailed information about the research approach or methods in a particular discipline.

Research approaches or paradigms

There are a number of different research approaches or paradigms, the two main ones being the subjectivist (sometimes called the interpretivist) approach and the objectivist (or positivist) approach. The approach taken by a researcher depends on their view of the world. In general, someone who takes a subjectivist or interpretivist approach uses qualitative methods to explore individual experiences and perspectives. In contrast, someone who takes an objectivist or positivist approach uses quantitative methods based on data that can be manipulated using statistical or other numeric methods. Research published in journals frequently does not explore the approach or paradigm that underpins the work, as it is implicit, and experienced researchers will be able to locate a particular study in terms of its underlying research approach or paradigm. However, research students are expected to explore and understand their underpinning research paradigm and this will involve them in discussing three sets of assumptions: ontological, epistemological, and human nature and agency. Table 2.1 outlines the two approaches.

Table 2.1 Overview of research approaches (adapted from Burrell and Morgan, 1979, as presented in Cohen, Manion and Morrison, 2000, 7)		
Assumptions	**Subjectivist approach**	**Objectivist approach**
Ontological	Nominalism	Realism
Epistemological	Anti-positivism	Positivism
Human nature and agency	Voluntarism	Determinism

Ontology

Ontology is concerned with the nature of the social phenomena being studied and it is typified by two positions: nominalist or realist. The nominalist position views the world as something that is socially constructed, and researching this world involves collecting subjective accounts and experiences, i.e. qualitative data. For example, my own research on students' experiences of e-learning takes a nominalist position, meaning that I believe that the world is socially constructed and my research process involves collecting accounts of individual students' experiences. In contrast, the realist position sees the world as given and separate from individuals; it can be researched through 'objective' data and involves using positivist, scientific and experimental methodologies, using quantitative data. A colleague of mine takes a realist position and his research involves using objective data collected through experiments and questionnaires. This dichotomy of nominalist and realist positions is an over-simplification, as even traditional realist approaches, such as scientific research, are socially constructed (Bryman and Bell, 2007).

Epistemology

The second set of assumptions is concerned with epistemology or the nature of knowledge. The positivist view is that knowledge is hard, objective and quantifiable, and research from this perspective involves 'objective' observers collecting and analysing quantitative data. The anti-positivist view is that knowledge is softer, subjective and based on individual experience; as a result, 'subjective' researchers must be taken into account during the development and implementation of a research project as their involvement in the project will have an impact on the research process and outcomes.

Human nature and agency

The third set of assumptions is concerned with human nature and agency, i.e. the perspectives either that individuals act voluntarily (voluntarism) or that their behaviour is predetermined (determinism), e.g. by instinct. Researchers who take the latter position are likely to select scientific approaches to research, involving experiments and measuring observations, while people who adhere to voluntarism are likely to use qualitative research methodologies and methods.

Selecting a research approach

New doctoral students often grapple with these ideas about the research approach and the concepts of ontology, epistemology and human nature. They may find that it takes some time to get to grips with such theoretical ideas, which are often the focus of elements of their programme. Once they have understood them, they must then decide on their own research approach. This is likely to involve considering the following:

- The dominant approach to research in their chosen field of interest. Using the same methodological approach as that commonly used by other researchers in the same field will help students to link their ideas and findings with those in the current research literature.
- The dominant approach in the organization or the context of study. For example, many research students in the health service work from a scientific or positivist perspective. This means that a health service manager may find that, by taking a scientific or positivist approach to research, the results are more likely to be accepted within the professional context than would be those of a subjectivist or interpretivist piece of work.
- Individual preferences, e.g. does the researcher want to carry out quantitative or qualitative research? If the researcher wants to perform qualitative research, this will involve a subjectivist

approach; and if quantitative research, then the approach will be objectivist (see Table 2.1, page 20).
- Advice and guidance from the doctoral student's supervisor.

Subjectivist

If a research student decides to take a subjectivist approach and carry out qualitative work, it is likely that the study will involve inductive reasoning (Figure 2.1 overleaf). This means that it will involve:

- identifying a research aim
- identifying research questions
- identifying the methodological approach
- data collection
- data analysis, resulting in the identification of patterns or trends
- development of tentative conclusions, including a possible theory.

Objectivist

If a research student decides to take an objectivist approach and carry out quantitative work, then the study is likely to involve deductive reasoning (Figure 2.2 overleaf). This means that the work will involve:

- identifying research aim
- identifying research hypotheses
- identifying the methodological approach
- data collection
- data analysis, resulting in testing the hypotheses
- development of tentative conclusions with respect to the original hypotheses.

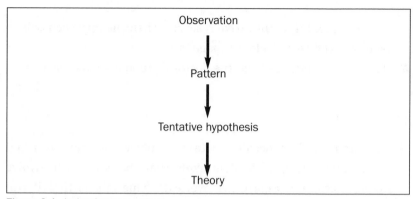

Figure 2.1 *Inductive reasoning*

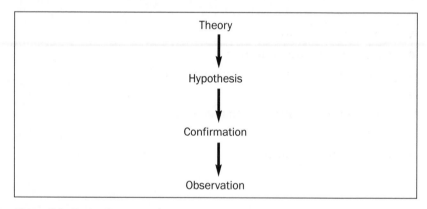

Figure 2.2 *Deductive reasoning*

Methodological approach

The term 'methodology' refers to the theory of acquiring new knowledge and the processes involved in identifying, reflecting upon and justifying the best research methods. Wellington (2000, 16) describes it as 'the activity or business of choosing, reflecting upon, evaluating and justifying the methods you use'. The research methodology involves considering the overall theoretical approach to the study and ensuring that it is in alignment with the research aims and questions (or hypotheses), the theoretical framework of the study and the underpinning literature base. If the research is in alignment with the specific field of knowledge in which it is located, then any knowledge generated is likely to be accepted by other researchers within the field and will contribute to the development of the knowledge base.

The next step is therefore to identify the methodological approach (of which there are many) that will be used. A selection of commonly used approaches is listed in Table 2.2, which categorizes them according to whether they are used in subjectivist or objectivist studies. Some methods, e.g. surveys, may be used in both types of research.

Table 2.2 *Different methodological approaches*	
Subjectivist	**Objectivist**
Action research	Experiments
Case studies	Historical research
Ethnographic research	Statistical approaches
Grounded theory research	Surveys
Historical research	Scientific methods
Surveys	

Action research

Action research is commonly used in disciplines, such as management and education, where practitioner researchers want to research the impact of their intervention(s) or innovations. A key feature of action research is that the researcher works in partnership with those being researched and the research process, including the findings, is shared with the participants. Action research typically involves a reflective process in which the researcher and participants reflect on the research and its outcomes, including its impact on them. Wisker (2001) describes action research as being 'practical, participative, emancipative, interpretative and critical'.

Case studies

A case study involves research that is located within a particular project, organization or context, and normally focuses on individuals or groups of actors and attempts to understand their experiences. Cohen, Manion and Morrison (2000, 181) write that:

> It provides a unique example of real people in real situations, enabling readers to understand ideas more clearly than simply by presenting them with abstract theories or principles. Indeed a case study can enable readers to understand how ideas and abstract principles can fit together. Case studies can penetrate situations in ways that are not always susceptible to numerical analysis.

Case study data is often 'strong in reality' and provides the reader with down-to-earth accounts, often supported by vivid descriptions of particular situations and illustrated with quotations. These may resonate with the reader's own experiences. Case studies provide an opportunity to explore in depth the complexities and subtleties of a particular situation. They are clearly located in the real world and the research findings may be used to change practice either in the specific case used in the research or in a related situation. One final advantage of case studies is that, in comparison with some research approaches, e.g. some quantitative studies, the findings from case studies are accessible and may be used by a wide range of people (Cohen, Manion and Morrison, 2000).

Ethnography

Ethnography was first developed by social anthropologists, who typically merged themselves into the day-to-day life of a particular group or culture. It is a commonly used approach both in educational research (Cohen, Manion and Morrison, 2000) and in business and management (Bryman and Bell, 2007), as well as in other fields in the social sciences. Ethnography is concerned with the 'real' world of everyday life, with the ways in which individuals make sense of their world and 'the assumptions they make, the conventions they utilize, and the practices they adopt' (Cohen , Manion and Morrison, 24). LeCompte and Preissle state that:

> Ethnographic research is a process involving methods of inquiry, an
> outcome and a record of the inquiry. The intention of the research is to
> create as vivid a reconstruction as possible of the groups or cultures
> being studied.　　　(Quoted in Cohen, Manion and Morrison, 2000, 38)

Ethnography involves the researcher in observing the social group that forms the focus of the research. The literature on this approach discusses the issue of participant observation. Bryman and Bell (2007) refer to the 1950s work of Gold, who identified four potential roles for ethnographic researchers, requiring different levels of involvement and detachment between the researcher and members of the social group, as represented in Figure 2.3 and as listed below:

- complete participant, where the researcher is a member of the social group, whose members are unaware that the research process is taking place
- participant-as-observer, where the researcher is a member of the social group and the members of the group are aware that the research is taking place
- observer-as-participant, where the researcher's role is chiefly that of interviewer but there is some interaction between the researcher and the members of the group
- complete observer, where the researcher does not interact with members of the group.

Involvement			Detachment
←			→
Complete participant	Participant-as-observer	Observer-as-participant	Complete observer

Figure 2.3 *Participant observer roles (adapted from Bryman and Bell, 2007, 324)*

Grounded theory research

Grounded theory is a qualitative research methodology that is commonly used in the social sciences. It is a research method in which theories are generated from data. This is in contrast to other research methodologies, e.g. scientific research, where the starting point is a theory, and data is then collected as a means of testing the theory. The starting point in grounded theory research is the collection of data using a range of different methods. The data is then coded using *de novo* coding, i.e. the codes are extracted from the data. Groups of codes are collected into concepts, and from these concepts categories are formed. The categories may then form the basis of a new theory.

Historical research

Research students who are carrying out historical research are likely to need access to a range of original documents, or their digital equivalents, in archive collections, in libraries and specialist research centres, in government agencies, or in the organization that is the focus of their research. These resources may include eyewitness evidence, including oral accounts. They will use these sources to explore their research question(s) or hypotheses. Some students will be performing quantitative historical research and will use original sources, e.g. medical records, to provide data for statistical analysis. Issues with which historical researchers are concerned include: authenticity and provenance of sources; historical reliability and issues of historical reasoning, including the structure and logic of historical arguments; and statistical inference.

Scientific methods

Scientific approaches to research are commonly used in health and also in some fields of psychology, as well as in the more traditional scientific subjects. The scientific research process results in the development of a body of knowledge or theory, and this has been tested by a number of different hypotheses. The basis of the scientific approach is that the researcher proposes a *hypothesis* or an explanation for some phenomena. On the basis of this hypothesis the researcher will make a prediction (a deduction), and this will be tested via an experiment. The scientific approach is based on the concept of objective data, and scientists are concerned that their experiments produce valid, reliable and generalizable results (these concepts are explored later in this chapter). Scientific experiments are often repeated in order to validate their findings.

Surveys

Surveys are used in both qualitative and quantitative research. Typically, researchers design surveys to collect data that will enable them to address their research hypotheses or questions. Questions may be open (where respondents are free to answer in their own words) or closed (where respondents must give a specific response, e.g. yes/no, true/false). Surveys may range in size from 10 to 100 questions (or even more), and research students may seek 100-plus respondents from the population that they are exploring. Nowadays, many surveys are carried out using electronic tools such as SurveyMonkey™ or ProQuest™. Research students conducting surveys to collect quantitative data will typically analyse their data using statistical tools such as SPSS™. In contrast, students who are more interested in collecting narrative may analyse their findings using text-based tools such as NVivo™.

Once the methodological approach has been identified, a research student is likely to want to read all the key textbooks on the subject. In addition, students find it helpful to read up-to-date journal articles and to study the methodological approaches used by current researchers. This helps to inform their study and to ground it in current research practice. Many research students use well known research methodologies in the same way as they are described in the standard textbooks and seminal works. Others find that using one methodology does not meet their research agenda, and they may need to develop their own approach involving 'mixed methods' or 'mixed genres'.

Data collection and analysis

At the heart of any research process are data and the collection of data. Researchers in different fields may collect data from a range of sources, such as experiments, animals and plants, people, computers or other systems. Commonly used data collection methods include scientific or psychological experiments, questionnaires, interviews, focus groups, data available via computer systems, original sources (e.g. historical or organizational documents), research diaries and learning journals. Researchers need to think through their research process and to design detailed data collection methods so as to make sure that the data collection method enables them to fulfil the aims of the study and of the research questions or hypotheses.

Qualitative data analysis

Once the researcher has collected her data, the data analysis process is likely to involve identifying general patterns or themes in that data. A helpful starting point is to skim through the data and become familiar with it and to start identifying general themes. Many researchers use coding systems to classify the data into categories and make sense of it. There are two distinct approaches to content analysis: *de novo* analysis, in which codes are developed from the data itself; and the use of a pre-determined coding scheme.

Many qualitative researchers use software packages to help organize and analyse their data, a commonly used example being NVivo™. NVivo™ accepts a wide range of data, including text-based documents, video files and media clips, audio files and digital photos and pictures. The software allows the researcher to search and code the data and then to categorize it. It has advanced database and classification tools and is able to handle thousands of documents or files.

The next stage in the research process involves what Radnor (2001) calls 'analysis to interpretation' and it is concerned with interpreting the findings and developing meaning from them. The first stage may involve writing statements that summarize the data as organized into categories (as outlined above). These are then worked with and used to develop an explanation of the findings.

Quantitative data analysis

The most common approach to quantitative data analysis is through the use of statistical methods and computer packages such as SPSS™. This involves inputting the data into the package and then manipulating it using standard statistical measures. Once the results have been obtained, they need to be interpreted and related to the original hypotheses.

A number of different groups of statistical methods are used by researchers. The first is called 'descriptive statistics' and they enable researchers to describe the characteristics of the data. Descriptive statistics includes common measures such as the mean, mode, standard deviation and range. Qualitative researchers sometimes use descriptive statistics by as a means of providing an overview of their data. Inferential statistics enable researchers to manipulate data, to test their hypotheses and to determine whether their results are statistically significant or have occurred by chance. Examples of tests used in inferential statistics include the Student's T Test, the Chi-Square Test, and Pearson's Chi-Square Test. In contrast, correlation and regression analysis enable researchers to explore the relationship(s) between different variables. Examples of correlation tools include the Pearson Product-Moment Correlation and the Rank Correlation. Examples of regression analysis statistical tools include the Analysis of Variance and the Analysis of Covariance. A critical aspect of identifying the appropriate research tools includes understanding and selecting the appropriate statistical measure.

Access and ethical issues

An important issue in all research studies and projects is that of obtaining access and ethical clearance. Universities and faculties have their own policies and practices regarding these matters. In general, researchers must put in an application to an ethics committee for clearance before they can start the research process. If the research is to take place in an organization, the researcher will need to obtain permission and ethical clearance from that organization. For example, for a study in an organization where the researcher is an employee, she will need to obtain the written consent of the appropriate managers or directors. In some organizations, e.g. the NHS, researchers need to apply for ethical clearance to carry out their research. This process may take a long time, e.g. six months, and researchers need to build this time into their action plan.

The internal ethics process in universities normally requires the researcher to complete a standard set of forms and to provide an outline of what she intends to do and of how the research activity meets the required ethical standards. This means that the researcher needs to consider ethical issues and to work out how to ensure that the research meets the required ethical standards. Common issues include data storage, ensuring the maintenance of participants' confidentiality and anonymity, and informed consent. When considering the data collected in the study, researchers need to reflect on how to keep it secure, e.g. in a locked cabinet, or accessible only via passwords in a computer. They also need to think about how to separate data identifying individuals from the completed questionnaires, interviews or data obtained from focus groups.

Informed consent

Another issue in research involving people is that of informed consent. There is a danger that gaining consent may be treated as a simple procedure of asking participants to complete and sign an 'informed consent form'. Rather, researchers need to ensure that their participants have a good understanding of what they are agreeing to and that they may withdraw from the research at any time. Many researchers provide a draft copy of their work to the participants, who then have the opportunity to suggest changes or amendments to the information that they have provided before a final version is produced. If researchers intend to carry out an experiment or to work with children or vulnerable adults, it is likely that they will need to gain special permission. Similarly, research activities involving animals also require additional permissions before the research can be started.

Researchers also need to consider how they will work with any participating third-party organizations, and this involves negotiating a range of issues, such as working practices, confidentiality, informed consent, intellectual property etc. Important issues that need to be resolved include: whether or not the researchers need to maintain the organization's anonymity in their work; who has access to the research; and intellectual property rights. A third-party organization may ask researchers to sign a non-disclosure agreement covering issues of confidentiality and publication and practices with respect to their competitors or any future employers for whom the researchers may work. Finally, universities, through their central services, normally provide specialist advice to researchers on carrying out research or projects with third-party organizations.

Summarizing the research process

Figure 2.4 summarizes the different levels of thinking and activity that take place during the research process. Researchers will work through this process in different ways. Experienced researchers may move quickly through the initial stages of the research approach, logic and methodology, as they are well established in their field and know their preferred research approach or paradigm, and also their research methodology and methods. In contrast, new researchers, including research students, may spend some time working through the different layers of the process. They are likely to start at the top level of the diagram, with either a subjectivist (interpretivist) approach or an objectivist (positivist) approach and then work down the different levels of Figure 2.4. Using this approach helps to ensure that their work is logical and internally consistent.

However, it is worthwhile remembering that this is a simplification of the research process and you are advised to read research methods textbooks so as to develop your knowledge of research with respect to any specific discipline.

Research issues

In all research studies or projects there is a need to ensure that the

Positivist	RESEARCH APPROACH ↓	Interpretivist
Deductive	RESEARCH LOGIC ↓	Inductive
Scientific experiment Survey	RESEARCH METHODOLOGY ↓	Action research Case study Ethnographic research Grounded theory research
Questionnaire Interview Experiments Observation	DATA COLLECTION METHODS ↓	Questionnaire Interview Focus groups Use of text Observation
Statistical methods Other numerical methods	DATA ANALYSIS METHODS	Descriptive statistics Textual analysis Discourse analysis

Figure 2.4 *Summary of research ideas*

work is carried out to an acceptable standard or quality. In traditional research projects some standard approaches are used to produce good quality research, and different measures are used for qualitative and quantitative projects.

Researchers who are carrying out a qualitative study often consider issues of credibility, transferability, dependability and confirmability (Bryman and Bell, 2007).

- *Credibility* relates to producing a credible account of the subject of the research. This involves producing an accurate account and one that is not made up, selective or distorted. Another aspect of producing a credible account relates to whether or not the study fairly represents the perspectives of different people and stakeholders relevant to the study.
- *Transferability* relates to the possibility of transferring the findings from the specific qualitative study to other situations.
- *Dependability* involves validating findings and ensuring that there is an audit trail. Using a range of different data sources will help to produce dependable findings and hence to build up an accurate picture of the focus of the study.
- *Confirmability* relates to the idea that the researcher has taken appropriate steps to ensure that she does not affect the research outcomes, e.g. as a result of individual beliefs or interests.

Researchers who are involved in quantitative studies consider issues of validity, reliability, and generalizability (Bryman and Bell, 2007).

- *Validity* is concerned with ensuring that the research is 'accurate' or 'truthful', e.g. have the researchers measured what they said they would measure? Have they used appropriate methods to select their sample? Is the sample of an appropriate size? What sources of bias may be in the study? How have these been addressed?

■ *Reliability* is concerned with consistency and replicability. If another researcher carried out the same study using the same methods in a similar context, would the same results be produced as those arrived at by the first researcher?

■ *Generalizability* relates to the idea that the findings from positivist research can be generalized to other situations or contexts.

One technique for ensuring that quantitative research is valid and reliable is through 'triangulation', which involves using multiple data sources as a means of creating an accurate account of the research (Bryman and Bell, 2007).

This section has provided a simple overview of the different concepts used in the research process. In reality, the process is much more complicated than indicated here and you are advised to use specialist textbooks on research methods relevant to particular disciplines if you require additional information.

Writing up

Researchers write up their work as it progresses. The starting point for many studies is a proposal or a bid, which provides an initial record of the research intentions. Throughout the research process, researchers will capture and record their work using a range of tools, e.g. research diaries, laboratory books, audio and video tape, e-mail. These working documents and resources often provide the starting point for writing up the research as an academic paper, a report (e.g. for the sponsoring organization) or a thesis. As explained in Chapter 1, many researchers present their initial findings at conferences, where feedback from their peers helps them to develop their work for publication in academic journals. This enables the knowledge created in the research to be disseminated, as described in more detail in Chapter 1.

The complexity of the research process

Although this chapter has presented the research process through a linear sequence of ideas, the reality is that individuals' research processes are often much messier, and represent an iterative process. I will explain this using my doctoral research, which was on the topic of e-learning and e-mentoring, as a case study.

In my research I took a subjectivist or interpretivist approach, as I was interested in exploring the actual experiences of students, mentors and tutors involved in a specific project. I did not think that taking a quantitative approach would help me to develop a deep understanding of the process. I believed that using a qualitative approach would enable me to explore and understand the experiences of students, mentors and tutors in a manner that would generate new knowledge and understanding that might then be applied to professional practice.

My research was located in domains of knowledge, i.e. learning and teaching, and management learning, where there is an established literature and research base that is underpinned by an interpretivist approach. I hoped that this would enable the research to be integrated into and help to develop existing knowledge domains. In addition, the project that was the basis of the study was developed using social theories of learning that are underpinned by a subjectivist approach. Consequently, taking a subjectivist approach in my own study aligned it with the underpinning basis of the project. In other words, my research approach was logically consistent with the subject under study.

My reasons for selecting my research approach, i.e. interpretivist, were very much based on my previous research experience and interests, and on my knowledge of the e-learning and e-mentoring literature. Having decided on this approach, I back-tracked and read the literature on educational research to help me to articulate and justify my approach. My next idea was to carry out a case study, and I explored this approach through an assignment earlier in my EdD studies. I stayed with this idea and, as a result of reading a number of textbooks as well as of original research, I realized that as I worked on the e-learning and e-mentoring project I needed to broaden the scope to include my own role as participant-as-observer. This realization led me to explore the literature on ethnography and to reframe my study as an ethnographic case study.

In terms of data collection I was aware that I would have access to a wide range of data sources, including project and mentoring evaluation documentation, e.g. project plans, steering group meeting minutes, project team meeting minutes; online discussion group messages; online module questionnaires; interviews; and my research diary. As the research progressed, I realized that I would have vast amounts of data to analyse and decided to use the computer software NVivo™ in the analysis process. Part of my motivation for using NVivo™ was to learn how to use it so that I would develop my research skills. Using this software enabled me to carry out content analysis and metaphor analysis of the data.

Issues of ethics and access are presented mid-way through this chapter, but in reality they are normally considered in the early stages of the research process, i.e. at the research proposal stage. In my own research, I completed ethics application forms at the very start of the research process, for both the university where I was enrolled as a student and my employing university where the project was located. The issues relating to qualitative research, the concepts of credibility, transferability, dependability and confirmability are presented towards the end of this chapter, but in reality, researchers are often concerned with them from the very start of the research process, and this was certainly my experience. I continually reflected on them, throughout the research.

This example taken from my own doctoral experience indicates that the research process is not linear but iterative, and that it is perhaps best represented as a spiral, in which issues are considered and reconsidered as the research progresses. In addition, the decisions made about the research process, i.e. the choice of research approach or paradigm, the research methodology and methods, and the approaches used to collect and analyse data are not based on theoretical grounds alone. These decisions are made as a result of current practices within the discipline, personal preferences and experiences, and pragmatism, e.g. consideration of the amount of time and resources available to carry out the research. Research that is funded externally will also be influenced by the needs of the funding body.

Summary

In this chapter I have provided an overview of the research process and have highlighted common approaches to research. This means that the chapter has not provided an exhaustive account of research approaches and methodologies. I have considered different styles of research, ranging from positivist to interpretivist, and have considered different research methodologies including: action research, case studies, ethnographic research, grounded theory research, historical research, scientific methods, and surveys. I have also considered data collection and analysis and issues of ethics and access, and have included a brief consideration of quality issues in both quantitative and qualitative research. Finally, I outlined the complexity of the research process and suggested that it is not a linear process, as suggested by the organization of this chapter, but an iterative one in which the researcher returns to the main decisions that she will make about her research at different stages in the research process. Lastly, it is worth noting that this chapter presents an overview and simplification of research and research processes. Each of the topics described here is the subject of active debate, and is supported by an extensive and specialist literature.

3

The research student's experience

Introduction

In this chapter I consider the role of the supervisor in the life of a doctoral student, and the early stages of the research journey. I cover the research process from getting started through to designing the process, including the topics of induction, working with a supervisor and getting started. Chapter 4 continues the research journey and explores the following stages: the literature review, methodology, fieldwork, writing up, the *viva voce* examination, amendments and completing the doctorate.

In this chapter I include examples from my own doctoral research experience and from colleagues who have been willing to share their experiences with me.

Starting points

The starting point for potential research students is a desire to continue their studies, e.g. to progress from a taught Master's degree to a research degree, or to return to academic life and complete a doctorate on either a full- or part-time basis, perhaps after a number of years in the workplace. As with students who want to join a taught degree programme, potential research students start their search for a suitable university and department on the basis of their field of interest, the reputations of individual researchers, departments and universities, the availability of funding (some universities provide bursaries and sponsored research studentships) and their desire to study in a particular city or country. There are many sources of information to provide them with advice, including websites such as those provided by the Research Councils (see Chapter 1) and sites such as:

www.findaphd.com/students/life.asp
www.vitae.ac.uk/
www.professionaldoctorates.com/

Useful textbooks on the subject, include: Gina Wisker's *The Postgraduate Student Handbook* (Palgrave Study Guide, 2001), and Estelle M. Phillips and Derek S. Pugh's *How to Get a PhD* (Open University Press, 3rd edition, 2000).

Once a student has identified an appropriate university, department and supervisor, he will be required to make a formal application to the university to become a research student. The application process varies from university to university, e.g. in some it is managed centrally by a graduate school or equivalent administrative unit, while in others research student applications are dealt with at faculty or department level. If the student is applying to undertake a PhD, it is likely that he will be required to write a research proposal as part of the application process. In contrast, students who are applying to study for a professional or practice doctorate may be asked to indicate their areas of interest, as they will work on their thesis proposals as part of the taught stage of the degree.

For many potential research students, the research proposal is an important document, as it will be used as the basis for deciding whether or not the student will be accepted by the university. The decision may be made at departmental level or by a research committee. Universities vary in the amount of help and support they provide to applicants who are required to write a detailed proposal.

The structure of a typical proposal is presented at the start of Chapter 2.

Writing a research proposal is a daunting task for many prospective students, especially for those who have been away from the world of universities for a number of years. One particular difficulty is that the student is required to demonstrate knowledge of the proposed research approach, methodology and methods before starting the research process, and these topics are often only covered in the taught skills modules that support research students at the start of their programme. In addition, an important part of the proposal covers the fact that the prospective student needs access to library and information sources in order to perform the literature review, but doesn't have access to these when not enrolled as a student at the specific university. Many academics are alert to these issues and read research proposals with an awareness of the contexts and limitations within which they have been produced. However, many students find it difficult, and it can create some negative feelings in relation to access to library and information resources, which individuals carry with them when they enrol as research students.

Once the student has been accepted on a research degree, he will be sent general guidance about university life, which is likely to include:

- a general guide including maps
- how to access university library and computer systems
- guides to university support services such as:
  — library and information service
  — advice on how to study
  — language support
  — accommodation
  — international student support services
  — finance
  — counselling services
  — careers services

— disability services.
- information about the students' union
- information about sports opportunities
- information about volunteering or other community opportunities
- university rules and regulations, e.g. on student discipline, assessment, computers.

Induction

Different universities organize induction for research students in different ways. In general, there will be activities organized at university level, perhaps by a graduate school, and also at departmental or faculty level. New international research students are likely to be invited to the general international induction programme, which often takes place during the week before the formal start of the semester. As with general induction for students on taught programmes, research students are likely to experience a range of welcome talks and lectures on different aspects of university life, including library and information services. They will also have opportunities to meet their supervisor, other researchers and new and continuing research students, through both formal sessions and informal social events. Feedback from research students about induction suggests that it varies from university to university, but in general students often feel that they are at the receiving end of too much information, thrust at them over a very short period of time. International students, who may be experiencing culture shock, may end up feeling confused and demoralized by the induction experience, rather than well informed and ready for their studies. This issue is explored in more detail in Chapter 6.

Many universities permit research students to enrol throughout the academic year and this means that students are likely to miss the formal induction events. Unless the university has special induction processes for these students, they may be left to discover vital information for themselves.

Working with a supervisor

For most research students, an important aspect of arriving at university is meeting their supervisor. The relationship between a research student and his supervisor is extremely important. Students normally have two supervisors. The first supervisor is usually allocated on the basis of the subject of the thesis, i.e. she is an academic with both expertise and an interest in the specific field of research. The second supervisor is often allocated on the basis of expertise in particular research methodologies or methods and general knowledge of the doctoral and university processes. Research students will first meet their supervisors during induction, although they may already have been in discussion with them, e.g. via e-mail, while working on their proposals.

An important first step is to build a professional working relationship and to establish a framework for meetings and the research journey. Individual supervisors will vary in their approach to working with students, from one meeting every few months (in accordance with the university regulations), to weekly progress meetings. A common pattern for meetings is monthly during the first year (as the student establishes the research process) and final year (as the student is writing up), with less regular meetings during the intervening year(s). The focus of the meetings will vary, but in general will be on the different stages of the doctoral process as the student progresses through his research journey.

At the start of the supervisory process, supervisors are likely to help the student to:

- settle into becoming a research student and networking within the university and with other doctoral students
- establish a pattern of working with the supervisor
- identify the topic of research and the literature base
- identify the proposed research approach, methodology and methods
- consider issues of ethics and/or access

- identify research skills training activities
- take part in university and departmental research networking events.

During the middle stageof the process the supervisor is likely to help the student by:

- keeping in touch
- providing general and specific advice as required
- encouraging and supporting the development of good quality research skills
- promoting discussions that enable the student develop his ideas and gain a deeper understanding of the subject and research methodologies and methods
- encouraging the student to write up his work
- providing constructive and critical feedback
- encouraging the student to take part in professional networking events and conferences.

At the final stages of the doctoral journey, the supervisor is likely to:

- encourage the student to write and produce a good quality thesis
- provide detailed and timely feedback on chapters and the whole thesis
- provide encouragement and support during the writing process
- enable the student to be well prepared for the *viva* examination and provide support before and after the event
- encourage dissemination of the research findings via conferences and publications
- provide employment references.

Wisker, writing for postgraduate students, provides a helpful list of what research students can expect from supervisors:

- to supervise
- to read your work thoroughly and in advance
- to be available when needed
- to be friendly, open and supportive
- to be constructively critical
- to have a good knowledge of the research area
- to structure the supervision and ongoing relationship
- to know how to ask open questions, how to draw out ideas and problems and how to elicit information, even if the student finds communication difficult
- to have sufficient interest in their research to put more information such as reading, resources and contacts their way
- to encourage you to attend appropriate conferences and introduce you to others in their field
- to be sufficiently involved in their success to help you focus on directing your work later for publication, promotion or job.
  Wisker (2001, 36)

Common problems that arise from the student's perspective include:

- a supervisor not having sufficient knowledge about the subject
- a supervisor whose research interests and approaches are different from those of the student
- a supervisor who is not available, e.g. owing to other pressures of work
- different expectations about the doctoral process, e.g. supervisor wanting three-monthly meetings, while the student wants to meet more frequently, or the supervisor wanting to control the detail of the doctoral work so that it becomes the supervisor's work rather than that of the student
- different expectations about the relationship between supervisor and student, e.g. the supervisor seeing it as a facilitating process while the student wants the supervisor to lead the research process

- communication barriers due to age, class, race, gender and professional experience
- personality clashes
- a change in supervisor.

Individual students' experiences of working with a supervisor will vary, depending on the range of factors considered above. Here are some examples of students' experiences:

> My first supervisor left the university and I had to start again with a new supervisor. I found this daunting and was worried that it would delay me. I did have to spend some time talking to my new supervisor about my research and she threw in some ideas and approaches that were new to me. Once we got going then it seemed to work well. Looking back on the experience, I gained different things from each supervisor so overall it was good. However, it was very stressful at the time.

> My supervisor is great. He sees me regularly and is very helpful. I couldn't ask for a better supervisor.

> XXX, my supervisor, was too obsessed with his own research and he wanted me to work in his narrow field of research using his research methods rather than following my own interests. I think he was only interested in his own publications. In the end, I transferred to another supervisor and this worked well.

> My supervisor was very strict. We [all her research students] met up every Friday afternoon and discussed our progress during the week then we talked about next week's work. It was more like being at work in a research laboratory rather than being a student. But, she has a good record of success with PhDs so I'm just going with it.

Getting started on the doctorate

The starting point for many research students is a research skills training programme, and this subject is explored in more depth in Chapter 5. These programmes typically involve a menu of taught modules from which individual students select and study those modules relevant to their own development needs. The research skills training is likely to occur at the same time as the student is starting his individual research, although for some students, e.g. those enrolled on professional doctorates, the start of their individual research and thesis takes place after they have successfully completed Stage 1 or the taught part of their doctoral programme.

Selecting a topic

A crucial milestone for all research students is selecting their research topic. As explained at the beginning of this chapter, many research students, particularly those working towards a PhD, will have identified and explored their topic in the proposal which they made as part of their application to the university. For other PhD students, this process happens during the first or second semester of their studies, although for students on professional doctorates it may not take place until the second or even third year of their programme.

Selecting a topic involves identifying an academic theme that merits further research. This may be for a number of different reasons, such as curiosity, the need to explore or understand a particular problem, a desire to change professional practice, personal interest, a gap in the literature or the requirements of a sponsor. In general, once a student has identified a relevant topic he will start to narrow it down, and this involves carrying out a literature review, exploring possible methodologies and discussions with supervisors and peers.

The research literature often implies that selecting a topic is a one-off activity. In reality, the topic is likely to develop and evolve as the student performs the research. For some students, the topic is not finalized until they actually complete writing up their thesis.

Developing the study

Wellington et al. (2005) describe the overall process of developing the study as 'framing the research', and it is made up of three activities: developing a theoretical framework; identifying a focus; and then designing the research. Once a research student has identified his topic and been given the go-ahead by his supervisor to explore it, then he will need to develop his work through three processes, which occur consecutively and also repeatedly throughout the doctorate process. These three processes will be dealt with sequentially, although in reality a student may be grappling with all three at the same time.

Developing a theoretical framework

This is sometimes confused with carrying out a literature review and using the findings of the review as a means of locating an individual piece of research within a particular field or discipline, building on existing knowledge or identifying appropriate research method-ologies for a particular study. Research does involve all of these activities, but in many cases it also involves identifying an underpinning theoretical framework which will then be used as a means of structuring, discussing and critiquing the research findings. A simple example of research students selecting a theoretical framework would be of a student selecting a feminist perspective. If a student uses a feminist perspective, then he will need to identify and discuss the range of feminist perspectives that are commonly used in the literature, and identify the specific feminist perspective that will be used to frame his study. This will mean that he will be likely to use feminist methodologies and methods in the research design, and also focus on gender issues within the study.

Identifying a focus

Once the research student has identified the general topic of research, then he needs to identify the specific focus of the research. This process may take months or even years, and it is likely that the focus will change and develop during the research process. I have met research students who changed their topic during the first two years of their PhD programme, e.g. one student began studying learning styles in the context of schools and then changed her focus to researching the reliability and validity of different tools for measuring learning styles.

In my doctoral research, my general topic was 'e-learning and e-mentoring in the context of management development' and my focus was on 'the impact of time (from an organizational and individual perspective) on the learning experiences of students and mentors in an e-learning and e-mentoring project in a UK business school'. I developed my specific focus as a result of a number of factors, including:

- my own interest in time and in other individuals' perceptions of time
- my interest in e-learning and e-mentoring
- my reading of the literatures of time, e-learning and e-mentoring, which demonstrated that although there had been some research in this area it was not extensive
- my work on the e-learning and e-mentoring, project which provided me with access to appropriate data
- discussions with my supervisor.

It took me a year to narrow down and decide on the specific focus of my research, and during this time, as well as reading the research literature on time, e-learning and e-mentoring, I was also reading and designing my methodology, using research methods textbooks.

Once I had identified my specific focus I then developed the title, aim and research questions. These were written in a more formal academic language than that in which I presented the topic above. The title was 'Organisational temporal landscapes and individual timescapes: experiences of time in an e-learning and e-mentoring project in a UK University Business School'. My overall purpose in this study was to explore the temporal landscapes in a specific project (the EMPATHY Net-Works project) which provided e-learning and e-mentoring opportunities to enable participants to gain employment in the logistics and supply chain industries) and to illuminate the relationships between this landscape and the temporal experiences of project members. The main focus of the research was the question:

> What are the relationships between the temporal landscapes of the EMPATHY Net-Works project and the learning experiences of project members?

This question was explored through the following subset of questions:

1 What are the temporal landscapes of the EMPATHY Net-Works project and the business school?
2 What are the temporal experiences of the project members?
3 What are the relationships between the temporal landscapes of the project and its members?
4 How does the project temporal landscape help or hinder students' learning experiences?
5 How does the project temporal landscape help or hinder e-mentoring experiences?
6 What are the implications of these findings for facilitators and managers of e-learning and e-mentoring projects?

In addition to identifying the specific title, aim and research questions, I also identified the boundaries or scope of the research. I was basing my research on a specific project (EMPATHY Net-Works) that was located in a UK business school and this meant that I would not explore other e-learning or e-mentoring projects. I was interested in the subjective experiences of students and mentors with respect to time rather than in what they learned as a result of their involvement in the project, and so I did not explore individual learning outcomes. Narrowing the scope in this way helped me to maintain my focus and also helped to keep the research to a manageable size. Finally, I decided that I was not going to focus on project management aspects of the project, as this would broaden out the scope too much.

Designing the research

At the same time as a student is identifying the theoretical framework and the focus of his research, he is likely to be designing the study. This involves the process that was explored in Chapter 2 and it is likely to result in the production of a research proposal which will be very similar to proposals written to obtain external funding. It is likely to contain the following headings:

- Title
- Introduction, containing:
  - — Project aims and objectives or research aims and hypotheses/questions
  - — Problem or issue that is to be addressed
  - — context of the work (if appropriate)
  - — Scope of the work, e.g. what is going to be included and what is going to be excluded
- Relevant literature
- Context of the study (if appropriate)
- Proposed methodology
  - — Research approach
  - — Methodology
  - — Data collection methods
  - — Data analysis methods
- Issues of ethics and access
- Resource requirements (if appropriate)

■ Action plan
■ Initial list of references.

Different universities and doctoral programmes manage this stage in different ways. In the case of some students who had to submit a research proposal as part of their application, they may be asked to provide a revised version once they have had time to work with their supervisor, undertake research skills training and use a range of library and information resources. In contrast, students who are enrolled on a doctoral programme with a taught element may undertake a module that is devoted to producing a research proposal, and the assessment activity is likely to be writing a proposal and reflecting on the process. This was my experience, and my research proposal had the following structure:

Working title
Introduction
Context
The issue
Research aim and questions
Background to the researcher
Theoretical framework and literature review
Methodology
Access and ethical issues
Data collection and analysis
Issues
Action plan
Conclusion
List of references

One notable difference between my proposal outline and the generic one described above, and also in Chapter 2, is that I included a section on 'Background to the researcher', which outlined my educational and professional experiences, and also my personal interest in the topic of 'time'. This section was included in the proposal because in many disciplines within the social sciences, including education, it is now accepted that research cannot be disembodied and separate from the researcher, who is an integral element of the research process (Sikes and Goodson, 2003). The researcher's values and beliefs, life history and experiences will all have an impact on his research approach, methodology and methods. For the reader of a thesis or any subsequent publication, having access to this information about the researcher's positionality is useful because it helps to locate the research. For some research students, this reflexive approach to writing a proposal and, subsequently, the thesis can be difficult, particularly if they come from a discipline where their experiences of academic writing involve producing 'objective' accounts written in the third person.

Once the final proposal has been written and accepted by the supervisor it will form the basis for the student's research. However, it is worth emphasizing that a proposal is a statement of intent, and for many students their research will develop as it progresses and it may end up being different from the original plan. This is all part of the doctoral student's research journey, which includes dealing with change and uncertainty.

Summary

In this chapter I have considered the role of the supervisor in the research process. I also outlined the starting processes for a research student, from applying to university through to the design of the research process. I have covered topics such as: starting points, induction, working with a supervisor and the overall process of developing the study or framing the research, which is made up of the three activities of developing a theoretical framework, identifying a focus and designing the research. The next chapter considers the remaining stages in the doctoral student's journey.

4

Moving forward and completing the research

Introduction

In this chapter I provide an overview of the research process, involving working on the thesis through to completing and obtaining a doctorate. This chapter covers topics such as: the literature review, methodology, fieldwork, writing up, the *viva* oral examination, amendments and completing the doctorate. As explained in Chapter 3, the final research proposal will have been developed, possibly throughout the first year of the doctoral programme for PhD students, and perhaps as a result of a taught module for students completing a professional or practice doctorate.

This chapter is illustrated with examples from my own doctoral research experience and from colleagues who have been willing to share their experiences with me.

Moving forward

Once the research student has developed her study by identifying the theoretical framework, identifying a focus and designing the research, then she is ready to progress her thesis. In the initial stages this is likely to involve further work on the literature review, more in-depth reading of the research methodology literature, and planning the field work or experiments. This period of the research process may take a year or even more, and it is likely that the student will revise the focus of her research, her methodology and her methods. Planning the fieldwork or experiments may also lead to further changes in the research process. For example, a student may find that she does not have access to a particular organization, or that her original plans were too ambitious to translate into a real-life experiment and that they need to be amended.

The literature review is a central part of a doctoral thesis, and Wellington et al. *(2005, 73)*suggest that it enables students to:

- define what the field of study is, by identifying the theories, research, and ideas with which the study connects
- establish what research has been done which relates to the research question or field of study
- consider what theories, concepts and models have been used and applied in the field of study
- identify and discuss methods and approaches that have been used by other researchers
- identify the 'gaps' or further contribution that the present piece of research will make.

The literature review process actually starts when the student begins to work on her thesis, e.g. when she produces her proposal, identifies her theoretical framework, focus and research methodology, and it continues until she has completed both writing up the work and her *viva voce* examination.

Working on the literature review may be a difficult process for research students. The diverse nature of this group of students means that some may have had little previous experience of carrying out a literature review and may be unfamiliar with basic academic research tools, i.e. abstracting and indexing services, the differences between primary resources (such as journal articles, research reports and theses) and secondary resources (such as textbooks). Also, students may not be familiar with using advanced search techniques.

Further, those research students who have been involved in professional practice for a number of years may have little experience of using a modern library and electronic information sources. In contrast, some research students will have high-level information skills and may need only a small amount of additional help and support with their literature reviews. In addition, the literature search and review may result in from 100 to 500 references for the final thesis, which means that students need to be able to manage their information effectively, e.g. by getting to grips with specialist software such as RefWorks™ or EndNote™.

Wellington et al. (2005, 82) suggest that research students find it helpful to use visual images to represent their literature review and they identify four different ways of structuring and explaining the literature and its relevance to a particular study. These four approaches are:

- *Zooming*. Here the student starts from a very general perspective and moves through the literature to the specific focus of the study.
- *Finding intersections*. In this case, the student explores three or four areas of literature and then focuses on the common ground in the middle.
- *Patch-working*. The student explores a wide range of topics and then links them together or 'weaves' them into one coherent 'story'.
- *Funnelling*. This is very similar to zooming and involves moving from the general to the specific.

The existence of at least four approaches to organizing a literature review, with other variations presented in specific journal articles, sometimes causes anxiety for research students, who want to know 'What is the right method of working on and writing up the literature review?'. There is no 'right' method, only the approach that is appropriate for the specific study. If information skills trainers offer a single approach to carrying out and writing up a literature review, this may cause anxiety among some research students who lack the confidence and academic skills to see that their work does not fit that particular model.

My own experience of working on the literature review for my doctoral thesis involved a mixture of zooming and patch-working. I started my literature search at a general level, focusing on four themes: time, e-learning, mentoring and student experiences. This helped me to narrow my search, and I wrote it up as a patch-work or jigsaw of topics which were linked by their relevance to my research aim and questions. Figure 4.1 shows the topics that I included in my literature review, which spanned three chapters: time and contemporary research; the context of the project, e-learning and e-mentoring; and the theoretical framework.

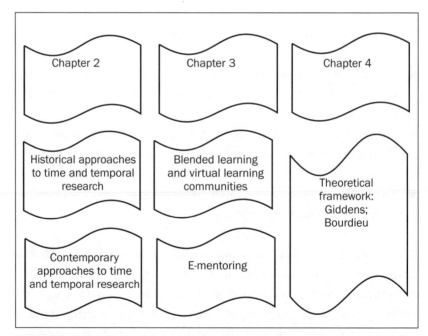

Figure 4.1 *Example of patch-working in a literature review*

In writing up the literature review, the student will be involved in a number of processes, such as:

■ identifying the main ideas and works relevant to the topic
■ synthesizing and making sense of the existing literature
■ critiquing existing research
■ explaining the relevance to the specific research that is being carried out.

Most students have no major problems with identifying the main ideas and works relevant to their topic. However, a number of students find it difficult to draw boundaries around their work and are unable to distinguish between primary sources that are highly relevant to their research and those that are tangential to it. This is one of the areas where the supervisor is important and these kinds of issue are often resolved in supervision sessions. Similarly, some students find it difficult to synthesize and make sense of the existing literature. Approaches that are helpful in this process include students making brief presentations to each other and their supervisor, as this helps them to summarize and make sense of their findings. In addition, questions from their audience or critical friends may help them to identify gaps or weaknesses in their approach.

A common problem arises with critiquing the literature. Wellington et al. *(2005, 84)*describe criticality as involving:

■ healthy scepticism . . . but not cynicism
■ confidence . . . but not 'cockiness' or arrogance
■ judgement which is critical . . . but not dismissive
■ opinions . . . without being opinionated
■ having a voice . . . without 'sounding off'
■ being respectful . . . without being too humble or obsequious
■ critical evaluation of published work . . . not serial shooting at random targets
■ being 'fair': assessing fairly the strengths and weaknesses of

other people's ideas and writing . . . without prejudice
- having your own standpoint and values with respect to an argument, research project or publication . . . without getting up on a soap box
- making judgements on the basis of considerable thought and all the available evidence . . . as opposed to assertions without reasons
- putting forward recommendations and conclusions, whilst recognizing their limitations . . . without being too apologetic.

This is a helpful list, though rather long. Many students find that a useful starting point for writing a critical literature review is to consider what each article adds to the field, the strengths and weaknesses of the particular research and its relevance to their own research. Reading the literature reviews in journal articles and general reviews of a particular field often provides a useful starting point to reading other people's research in a critical manner. Avidly reading discussion sections in journal articles often provides helpful pointers for approaches to criticality, as the author may well critique his own work. Finally, talking about the literature review and describing and critiquing other people's research, e.g. in seminars, often helps students to clarify their ideas and to 'find their own voice' with respect to their subject.

It is worth noting that the literature review continues throughout the whole research process. Even as a student is preparing for her *viva voce* examination it is likely that she will keep up to date with the literature in her specific field. However, some students find it difficult to stop working on their literature reviews because they are anxious about possibly missing a key journal article. This anxiety may prevent them from moving beyond the literature review in their doctoral research. However, if the student's general search strategy is effective, this is unlikely to be the case, and all students need to decide when to draw a line under their study with respect to published research.

Methodology

The next stage in the research process involves developing and putting into action the research methodology. Chapter 2 provides a general introduction to research approaches and paradigms, methodologies and methods. It also highlights the importance of access and ethical issues in research. Having completed the literature review, the research student may decide to amend the methodology that was outlined in her proposal. This stage of the research journey often occurs at the same time as the literature review.

Fieldwork

Many doctoral students carry out some kind of data collection process. This may involve scientific or psychological experiments, questionnaires, interviews, focus groups, data available via computer systems, using original sources – e.g. historical or organizational documents – or research diaries and learning journals. This process may take place in the laboratory, on campus, in the workplace or in some other location. Many students perform their field work in another country. During the fieldwork part of the research, students typically focus on the data collection and analysis process, rather than on other aspects of their work such as the literature review or writing up.

For many students, their fieldwork is an enjoyable and satisfying experience. It may require many hours of work, but, equally, students are likely to have a sense of moving forward with their research. However, for some students the fieldwork stage may throw up new challenges, e.g. a student may have arranged to carry out interviews with colleagues in her home country but then find that family issues cause difficulties and delays resulting in changes to travel plans and postponement of scheduled research activities. Sometimes a student may find that there has been a change of government, administration or management, resulting in the withdrawal of permission gained earlier in the research process, and this may necessitate a change of research focus, or identification of a different source from which to obtain their data and getting permission to do so.

If a student is working off campus during her fieldwork she may have limited access to e-mail and the internet. This may be the source of some frustration and it may limit her work. However, many students will have access to these tools while they are performing their fieldwork, and this means that they may be in contact with their personal supervisor, library and information workers, and other research students. Chapter 6 considers the development of virtual graduate schools, which provide a vital resource and support mechanism for research students.

Writing up

The production of the thesis and its examination is at the centre of the research student's experience. Ideally, students will be engaged in writing throughout their research, as it is an integral part of the thinking process. The process of writing helps to clarify thinking. The initial stage of putting ideas on paper helps the student to understand the research and, possibly, to identify weaknesses and areas that need further work. The process of returning to a draft and rereading it, plus gaining feedback from others, helps the student to identify ways in which it can be improved. Elbow (1973) describes this generative model of writing as involving two processes: growing and cooking. Growing involves the production of initial drafts, while the cooking process involves rereading, feedback from others and rewriting.

Some research students find it difficult to know where to start their writing process. It is helpful that they probably won't need to start with an empty screen or blank sheet of paper, as many documents produced as part of the research process will contribute towards the final thesis, and these earlier works help the student to get started. Example documents include: the original research proposal, the research diary or learning journal, laboratory books, the literature review, papers and presentations prepared for the personal supervisor or for research seminars. In contrast, some students will prefer to start a fresh document.

Most students will plan the structure of their thesis and their supervisor is likely to ask for a plan at an early stage in the research process. The plan may be produced at the level of chapter headings, although some students (and supervisors) may prefer to produce a more detailed plan and outline the sections and subsections. Some students prefer to do their planning by making lists, while others prefer more visual methods, e.g. using techniques such as MindMaps™ or spider diagrams, or tools such as Post-it Notes™. Typical approaches to planning the work include:

- producing a general plan at the level of chapter headings
- producing a specific plan worked out to the level of sections and subsections
- producing a MindMap™ or spider diagram which identifies the main chapters and themes
- starting with one topic, e.g. literature review or methodology, and then letting the work develop, i.e. going with the flow.

Many students find that as their written work develops and matures they move away from their original plan.

Writing is an individual activity and many people find it difficult and a real struggle. There are three main reasons why people find writing such a challenge (Wellington et al., 2005). First, many people lack confidence in their writing skills because of lack of experience, uncertainty about the requirements of academic writing, English being their second language, or concerns about their grammar and spelling. Second, writing up a thesis is challenging because it involves learning, which is sometimes a painful and messy process, as well as a motivating and liberating one. Carrying out research is not a linear process that involves doing the research and then writing it up. Instead, the writing process starts at an early stage and is an intrinsic part of the research journey, involving learning, and many people learn as they think about what they write. Third, writing is a difficult process because it takes time and energy to produce good quality text which accurately expresses what the author wants to say. My own experience is that it is like developing a garden, and once I have got the basic design worked out it is then a matter of working on each section time and time again, and doing this over time, i.e. in different seasons, when it is possible to gain different perspectives, and also of asking critical friends for their feedback. Producing a beautiful garden, like a well written thesis, requires lots of time and attention to detail.

Different students will develop their own strategies for getting going and writing their thesis. Commons strategies include:

- writing at a time of day which suits them; for some students this may be early morning, while for others it will be in the evening
- finding a good environment for writing, and this will vary for different students: some people prefer quiet environments while others like to listen to music; some students prefer to write at home or in the library, while others prefer to write in a shared office
- writing anything as a way of getting started and not being too concerned about 'getting it right' first, second or even third time; this approach to writing involves seeing it as a generative activity which involves growing and cooking
- ending a writing session in the middle of a section rather than at the end of a section; this can help the author to get started on the writing process more quickly next time she sits down to write her work
- establishing and maintaining a writing momentum: students who have a week or more break between writing sessions often find that they have to spend a lot of time getting back into their work, and this is demoralizing; spending a shorter amount of

time writing on a more regular basis is often a more efficient and effective strategy.

Some students are concerned about the academic style of writing a thesis. Ideally, they will have access to theses available in the department, library or online repository and these will provide exemplars of good practice. There are two main styles of academic writing: the traditional approach involves using a serious and formal impersonal tone. It involves presenting different ideas and the evidence to support them. This means not writing in the first person (not using 'my', 'I', 'we') and presenting an objective and depersonalized approach. In some subjects, e.g. some education or management topics, it is acceptable to use the first person. If a student is unsure about which style to adopt, she needs to discuss it with her supervisor and also look at published work in her specific field of research.

The first completed draft of the thesis is only a starting point. Students will need to work on their initial draft and obtain feedback from their supervisor, and also from critical friends. In addition to the subject content, the work needs to be checked to ensure that:

- the thesis complies with the presentation requirements of the university
- headings and subheadings are meaningful and consistent
- diagrams, tables and figures are correctly and consistently labelled
- the reader is guided through the thesis, e.g. by the use of an introduction and summary or conclusion to each chapter
- all references are correctly listed and cited
- layout is visually pleasing and involves an appropriate use of 'white' space
- grammar and spelling are correct.

My own experience of writing up my thesis was that I kept a range of working documents, e.g. my proposal, initial literature review, a couple of PowerPoint™ presentations and a draft conference paper, and these provided a starting point. I worked out my structure, i.e. chapter headings and main themes, using Post-it Notes™ and this was approved by my supervisor. I then started writing Chapter 1 'Introduction'. As I completed each chapter, I sent it to my supervisor, who provided me with written feedback. He preferred me to send him a printout rather than an electronic version of the file and he annotated each chapter and returned it to me. Once I had completed the final chapter then I printed three copies of the complete thesis. I worked through one copy, my supervisor read another copy and a critical friend kindly agreed to give me feedback on the third copy. Once I had received the feedback and worked on it I produced my final version. I then submitted this to the university, following guidance on the university website to get it bound and submitted. This process took a year, and throughout this time I always worked to deadlines, e.g. I agreed to submit at least one draft chapter to my supervisor each month. This meant that I had to keep up quite a demanding pace, and to do so I worked four evenings a week from 8 p.m. to midnight and all day Sunday. I also spent my summer holiday of two weeks working on it. The speedy turnaround of the draft chapters and feedback from my supervisor were extremely motivating. This process worked for me because I had set my deadline and I focused on achieving it. I didn't want my doctoral programme to extend any longer, and decided that it was worthwhile giving up other activities and prioritizing my thesis for a year in order to achieve my goal.

Viva voce examination

The *viva voce* (literally, 'live voice') examination is an integral and crucial part of the doctoral process. The conduct of the examination varies from country to country. In many European countries it is a public examination, held in front of an audience which may include family and friends. In contrast, in the UK the *viva* is normally held in private and the candidate is likely to be examined by two academics (an internal and an external examiner), and the process will be managed by an independent chairperson. In the case of a candidate who is employed by the university in which she is a doctoral student it is likely that there will be two external examiners. In addition, the supervisor may be present in the role of an observer. The detailed conduct of the *viva* examination will be framed by the regulations of the specific university.

The purpose of the *viva* examination will depend on the actual regulations of the university and is likely to include some or all of the following objectives:

- testing the student's knowledge of her subject and research
- clarifying any queries about the thesis
- ensuring that the student has developed doctoral level research skills
- providing an opportunity for the student to defend her thesis
- checking that the thesis is the student's own work.

It is worth noting that although the *viva* examination plays an important part in academic rituals, i.e.; it is an important rite of passage for new academics, it is an examination. There are a number of possible outcomes, which will depend on the university's regulations. Typical outcomes include:

- pass
- pass with minor amendments
- pass with substantive amendments with/without another *viva*
- fail, but student is permitted to resubmit thesis with another *viva*
- fail and student is not permitted to resubmit.

Each university has its own procedures relating to the management of *viva* examinations. Typically, a *viva* will be organized about three months after the submission of the thesis. The date will be arranged in discussion with the student, who may also be asked to have input into the selection of the examiners. The examiners will each write an independent report on the thesis and then discuss their reports. The outcome of these discussions will help to frame the discussions and questions during the examination. The structure of the examination is likely to include the following:

■ introductions: candidate advised on structure of the *viva*
■ general conversation to help candidate settle down
■ a series of questions
■ candidate likely to be given the opportunity to add additional information
■ end of *viva*.

The meeting may last between one and six hours. Two to three hours is the most typical length of time. The procedure will ideally involve a professional, semi-structured discussion in which the candidate is able to share her knowledge of her subject and to justify her thesis, e.g. in terms of the literature review, methodology and findings. The process should enable the candidate to defend her ideas and to explain any aspects of the research that are not 100% clear to the examiners. At the end of the examination the candidate will be asked to wait while the examiners discuss their findings. The candidate will be invited back into the room and provided with informal feedback about her performance. A written report will be sent to the student several weeks later. Most supervisors will debrief their candidate after the oral examination and ensure that she understands what happens next.

For most research students the *viva* examination is a milestone, and one that often appears to be daunting. Students may approach it in a variety of states, ranging from confident to terrified. For international students, who may be examined in their second language, the thought of an oral examination may be especially daunting. Typically, students will spend weeks preparing for the examination and this preparation may involve rereading and summarizing their thesis, returning to key seminal papers on their topic, working through typical questions that may be asked, and perhaps taking part in a practice *viva voce*. During this time, a student may chase up references in the library and anxiously check information presented in her thesis.

Amendments and completion

A very common outcome from the *viva voce* examination is that the student has passed, subject to making amendments to the thesis. The level of amendments may vary from correcting a couple of typographical errors and inaccurate references to having to rewrite one or more chapters. Different students will approach the amendments in different ways: for some, it is a relatively simple job and they take a pragmatic approach to completing them in order to obtain their doctorate; in contrast, others may have had their confidence dented as their perception was that their thesis was 'perfect', and being asked to make amendments is a sign that they have not succeeded. The university will set a deadline for the resubmission of the amended thesis, which may be 3, 6 or 12 months. For some students, this is a difficult time as they may have started a new job, e.g. as a lecturer, which will bring with it new work pressures, but at the same time they need to finish their thesis. At this stage some students will be in contact with library and information workers as they may need to double-check references or find new ones. Once the thesis has been amended it will be resubmitted and, hopefully, meet the requirements of the examiners, and the student will be awarded a doctorate. After the doctorate is completed many students disseminate their findings via conferences, academic journals and the appropriate professional press.

Summary

Chapter 4 completes the review of the research journey typically experienced by doctoral students and introduced in Chapter 3. In this chapter I have covered topics such as the literature review, methodology, fieldwork, writing up, the *viva voce* examination, amendments and completing the doctorate.

5
Research skills training

Introduction

The purpose of this chapter is to identify the range of skills required by research students in order to enable them to successfully complete their individual research and obtain a doctorate. These include information skills, the ability to access and use different resources and skills for different stages in the doctoral journey. In addition, research students need to develop a range of skills that will enable them to obtain employment either as academics or researchers, or within particular professions. Research students, especially those studying for professional doctorates, may also need to develop their employability skills, e.g. to enable them to move from management to strategic roles.

Training and skills of research students

In the UK in recent years concerns and initiatives have been aimed at developing the skills base and employability of research students. In Chapter 1 it was noted that doctoral education has shifted its focus from providing an experience enabling entry into an academic community and career, to providing a qualification for entry into the wider labour market. This puts emphasis on doctoral students gaining a wider set of employability skills (Chiang, 2003) and contributing to the knowledge-based economies after graduation. The need was identified by the UK Research Councils, who, working in collaboration with Vitae, previously UK GRAD, and the higher education sector, developed the Joint Statement of Skills Training Requirements of Research Postgraduates in 2001. This initiative identified the competencies that a postgraduate researcher should develop during the course of his doctoral programme.

As part of this trend the UK government commissioned a review to investigate the supply of people with science, technology, engineering and mathematical skills (the STEM subjects). The outcome of the review was the report *Set for Success* (Roberts Review, 2002), which recommended a number of developments in doctoral education, including additional training for doctoral students and postdoctoral researchers. One of the outcomes of this influential report was that the UK government provided funding from 2003 for the development of professional and personal skills in doctoral students. This led to the implementation in universities of research skills and professional development programmes for research students. In addition, it helped to fund initiatives such as the virtual graduate school, which are presented in Chapter 7.

The UK Research Councils' Joint Statement of training requirements for research students

The UK Research Councils' Joint Statement (2001) provides a benchmark statement that will help universities to provide the highest standard of research training across all disciplines. It also helps to promote consistency across universities, in that all doctoral students should have access to research skills and wider development opportunities wherever their research is located in the UK. The Statement identifies the skills that doctoral research students should be expected to develop during their research training, but is not prescriptive in terms of the process for skills development. It states:

These skills may be present on commencement, explicitly taught, or developed during the course of the research. It is expected that different mechanisms will be used to support learning as appropriate, including self-direction, supervisor support and mentoring, departmental support, workshops, conferences, elective training courses, formally assessed courses and informal opportunities.

The Research Councils highlight the central importance of research skills training for doctoral students and suggest that the development of wider employment-related skills should not detract from the core objective of the doctoral programme, i.e. the development of researchers. The competencies identified in the Joint Statement are listed below and it is worth noting that individual research councils may add to this framework in order to address specific skills requirements within a specialist area.

(A) Research Skills and Techniques – to be able to demonstrate:

1   The ability to recognise and validate problems.
2   Original, independent and critical thinking, and the ability to develop theoretical concepts.
3   A knowledge of recent advances within one's field and in related areas.
4   An understanding of relevant research methodologies and techniques and their appropriate application within one's research field.
5   The ability to critically analyse and evaluate one's findings and those of others.
6   An ability to summarise, document, report and reflect on progress.

(B) Research Environment – to be able to:

1   Show a broad understanding of the context, at the national and international level, in which research takes place.

2   Demonstrate awareness of issues relating to the rights of other researchers, of research subjects, and of others who may be affected by the research, e.g. confidentiality, ethical issues, attribution, copyright, malpractice, ownership of data and the requirements of the Data Protection Act.

3   Demonstrate appreciation of standards of good research practice in their institution and/or discipline.

4   Understand relevant health and safety issues and demonstrate responsible working practices.

5   Understand the processes for funding and evaluation of research.

6   Justify the principles and experimental techniques used in one's own research.

7   Understand the process of academic or commercial exploitation of research results.

(C) Research Management – to be able to:

1   Apply effective project management through the setting of research goals, intermediate milestones and prioritisation of activities.

2   Design and execute systems for the acquisition and collation of information through the effective use of appropriate resources and equipment.

3   Identify and access appropriate bibliographical resources, archives, and other sources of relevant information.

4   Use information technology appropriately for database management, recording and presenting information.

(D) Personal Effectiveness – to be able to:

1   Demonstrate a willingness and ability to learn and acquire knowledge.

2   Be creative, innovative and original in one's approach to research.

3   Demonstrate flexibility and open-mindedness.

4   Demonstrate self-awareness and the ability to identify own training needs.

5   Demonstrate self-discipline, motivation, and thoroughness.

6   Recognise boundaries and draw upon/use sources of support as appropriate.

7   Show initiative, work independently and be self-reliant.

(E) Communication Skills – to be able to:

1   Write clearly and in a style appropriate to purpose, e.g. progress reports, published documents, thesis.

2   Construct coherent arguments and articulate ideas clearly to a range of audiences, formally and informally through a variety of techniques.

3   Constructively defend research outcomes at seminars and *viva* examination.

4   Contribute to promoting the public understanding of one's research field.

5   Effectively support the learning of others when involved in teaching, mentoring or demonstrating activities.

(F) Networking and Teamworking – to be able to:

1   Develop and maintain co-operative networks and working relationships with supervisors, colleagues and peers, within the institution and the wider research community.

2   Understand one's behaviours and impact on others when working in and contributing to the success of formal and informal teams.

3   Listen, give and receive feedback and respond perceptively to others.

(G) Career Management – to be able to:

1   Appreciate the need for and show commitment to continued professional development.

2   Take ownership for and manage one's career progression, set realistic and achievable career goals, and identify and develop ways to improve employability.

3   Demonstrate an insight into the transferable nature of research skills to other work environments and the range of career opportunities within and outside academia.

4   Present one's skills, personal attributes and experiences through effective CVs, applications and interviews.

This statement provides a framework for universities and other bodies in the higher education sector for the development of:

- training or learning needs analysis on induction and throughout the course of the doctoral programme
- personal development planning (PDP)
- a map for the provision of training and skills development in postgraduate research students.

This initiative has provided fresh opportunities for library and information workers to contribute to research training programmes within universities. Items 2–4 of Statement C are the areas where many library workers become involved in supporting research students. This is explored in more depth in Chapter 6.

Skills development

The research skills training provided to doctoral students will vary from one university to another. However, it is common for universities to provide generic skills training aimed at all research students, and also more specific training linked to the research activities of individual departments and faculties. These programmes are normally developed with an awareness of the UK Research Councils' Joint Statement (2001) outlined above. Typically, the training is organized and managed by a graduate school (or an equivalent cross-university unit) whose role is to manage the research skills programme and ensure that an appropriate range of modules is offered to research students.

Doctoral students are normally expected to take responsibility for their own research skills training, as illustrated in Figure 5.1, which is likely to involve them in the following activities:

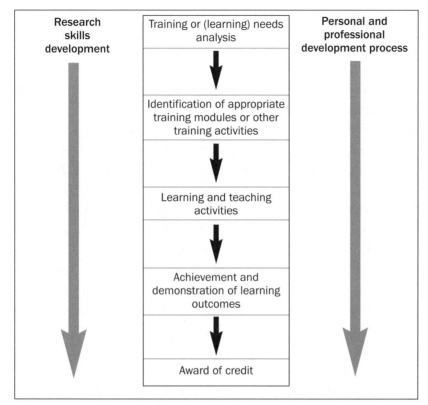

Figure 5.1 *Development process for research students*

1 Initial meeting with the student's supervisor and the completion of a Training Needs Analysis (TNA) or Learning Needs Analysis (LNA) – different universities use slightly different approaches and nomenclatures for this stage in the process. The TNA or LNA will form the basis of a Personal Development Plan (PDP) and helps to drive the student's research journey and training programme.

2 With the approval of their supervisor, students then sign up for the appropriate training modules or other development activities to enable them to develop an appropriate range of research and employability skills.

3 As with taught programmes, research students are required to engage with the relevant modules and complete the learning and teaching activities, as well as any assessment activities.

4   On successful completion of the modules students are awarded credit. The amount of credit awarded for research skills modules varies from university to university and is typically 10, 15 or 20 credits at Level 7.

5   Throughout the process, research students are expected to maintain their personal development folder. It is common for some of the activities they encounter to feed directly into their PDP.

It is worth noting that as students are undergoing the research skills training programme they will also have embarked on their individual research. Ideally, the training programme is organized in a timely manner so as to complement and enhance the student's research experiences. This means that some doctoral students who are also involved in part-time teaching or demonstrating work have a very busy schedule as they attempt to balance all the activities outlined in Figure 5.2.

As in the cases of undergraduate and taught postgraduate students, research students are encouraged to maintain their progress file (sometimes called a personal development folder or portfolio), which enables them to manage and record their personal development. It is a physical or electronic file where students maintain a record of:

■   transcripts of their credits for research skills training and information about individual modules successfully completed

■   individual personal development plans and records, including reflections on their learning, achievements, plans and goals

■   records of other achievements, e.g. papers presented at student conferences, information and feedback relating to teaching and learning activities

■   records of other activities, e.g. attendance at non-credit-bearing courses, internal conferences and seminars

■   a completed and up-to-date *curriculum vitae*.

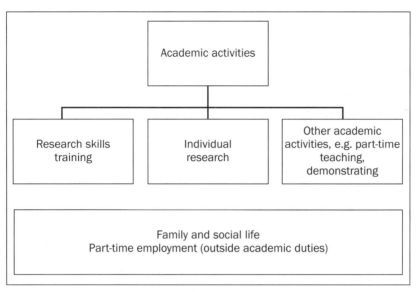

Figure 5.2 *Doctoral students' activities*

The portfolio may be used in a number of different ways, including:

- to keep a record of research and personal achievements and experiences
- for use in preparation for the *viva*
- to help in completing job applications and preparing for interviews.

A range of generic modules may be provided as part of the research skills training programme, typical examples including:

- Managing the research process
- Computer basics
- Computer data management
- Project management
- Research ethics
- Practical demonstration skills
- Library and information skills

- Career management skills
- Academic writing skills
- Writing the literature review
- The research interview
- Survey methods and questionnaire design
- Quantitative data analysis
- Using SPSS™
- Qualitative data analysis
- Discourse analysis
- Viva voce
- Writing for publication
- Introduction to teaching and learning
- Preparing and managing conference presentations
- Preparing and presenting conference posters.

In addition to generic modules, students will also have access to specific modules relevant to their research topics. For example, social science students are likely to be offered modules on topics such as ethnography and discourse analysis, while business and management students may have access to modules such as non-traditional qualitative research or multivariate analysis. There are normally restrictions on the number and type of modules an individual student may complete as part of his research skills training. It is possible to achieve an academic award for completing the modules, e.g. students who complete 60 credits are likely to receive a Postgraduate Certificate in Research Training and may use the letters PGCert after their name. Students who complete 120 credits receive a Postgraduate Diploma in Research Training and may use the letters PGDip.

Library and information research skills

An important and landmark publication by the Research Information Network (RIN) is their report *Mind the Skills Gap:*

information-handling training for researchers (RIN, 2008), which focuses on 'the nature, extent and organization of the information-related training provided by universities and other higher education institutions for researchers, and how that training is funded'. The authors explore and make recommendations on issues such as: the need for strategic management and co-ordination of information skills training both at institutional and UK levels; the role of libraries and library and information workers; and the importance of communication and co-ordination of research skills training across institutions. A full copy of the report is available at www.rin.ac.uk/training-research-info.

The RIN report recommendations include:

- Librarians and other information specialists, academic staff, and central training units should join in developing and delivering training programmes which recognise the strengths of different training approaches and techniques, and seek both to enhance understanding of the information landscape and to develop skills in the use of specific tools.
- All training programmes should be developed and where appropriate delivered in partnership with relevant members of academic staff, and should so far as possible take account of and exploit the experience and expertise already acquired by trainees; disciplinary differences and cultures; and differences in researchers' current roles and levels of experience.
- Libraries and other training providers should seek to exploit the potential of e-earning and blended learning approaches to training; but they should be cautious in seeking to avoid the many potential pitfalls in the way of constructing effective e-learning programmes.
- Libraries and other training providers should adopt more systematic and innovative approaches to identifying and assessing the needs of researchers to enhance their information-related skills and competencies.

■ Libraries should review the capacity and the capabilities of their staff in providing, in partnership with academics and others, high-quality training that will be valued by researchers; and they should avoid any temptation to oversell what they can offer.

(RIN, 2008)

These recommendations are helpful as they highlight the importance of library and information workers becoming engaged in inter-disciplinary team work across universities and other higher education institutions to develop and deliver high quality inform-ation training.

The development of research skills training programmes and generic modules provides an excellent opportunity for library and information services to become involved in the development of doctoral students, one approach being for the library or information service to provide a taught module. An example of such a training module is provided by the University of Hull, and the details are presented in Example 5.1. Further examples of information skills provision are presented and discussed in Chapter 6.

Example 5.1 Taught module

Module title: Library and Information research skills by independent study

Content and aims

The module aims to ensure that students are (a) aware of the electronic and printed information resources appropriate to their subject area and accessible in the University that will enable them to find good quality information, and that they can (b) search these effectively and (c) evaluate what they find. It also aims (d) to give awareness of the services and help available in the University's Libraries. The module is designed for independent study and thus aims to be suitable for all research students, on or off-campus, full or part-time.

Learning outcomes

On completing this module, students will be able to

- recognise that what are the most appropriate sources of information will vary depending on their subject and their needs
- select the most appropriate information resources for topics in their research area, with regard to their subject and their needs
- formulate a search for information, identifying relevant keywords and combining these in an effective search strategy
- apply well-formulated search strategies effectively and appropriately to different kinds of information resources, including indexes to theses, indexes to periodical articles, full text electronic journal services, library catalogues, web search engines, and subject gateways of evaluated web resources
- critically evaluate the results of a search for information in terms of a range of criteria
- reference accurately a range of different kinds of information using an appropriate format
- make effective use of the services and help available in the University's Libraries.

Mode of delivery

This module is delivered online using the university's virtual learning environment.

The involvement of library and information staff in the delivery of these taught modules often provides useful opportunities for networking and influencing the whole of the research skills training programme, as well as becoming involved in other aspects of support for doctoral students.

Case Study 5.1: Use of information sources

As part of their research skills development students are required to develop their knowledge and skills in identifying and using information sources. This case study is based on investigations by Chu and Law (2006), who describe the six types of information source used by research students:

Research-oriented sources
    Refereed journals, review articles, books, free web sources,
    bibliographies, conference papers, theses.
Contact with the research community
    Student's supervisor, outside experts, attending conferences, online
    discussion groups.
Bibliographic support sources
    Library and information workers, interlibrary loan, other local libraries,
    reference librarians.
Professional sources
    Technical reports, standards, patents, trade journals.
Academic tool books
    Thesis writing guidebooks, books on studying for the PhD,
    encyclopedias.
Media and statistics
    Newspapers, magazines, government publications, statistical sources.

Chu and Law's study focused on the needs of engineering and education students. The first category of information resource, research-orientated sources, was identified by all the students surveyed as the most important of six groups of sources.

Changing information needs

Chu and Law explored the changes in students' needs over time. They found that the main concern of research students was to become experts in their specific fields, that students were initially novices both in their field of research and with respect to information skills, and that as their subject expertise developed, so did their information searching skills. In addition, they found that students' information needs changed over time from general to specific. At the start of their research, students required general information to help them develop their understanding of a specific field. Once they had this broad understanding they then wanted more specific information to help them understand their particular field. This development process from general to specific information needs was then followed by a requirement to access up-to-date information, e.g. through online discussion groups. This shift in information needs is reflected in Figure 5.3.

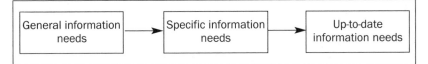

Figure 5.3 *Research students' changing information needs*

Chu and Law also investigated how research students' needs for different types of information source in the six categories changed during their research and as they developed both their specific subject knowledge and their information skills.

Research-oriented sources

In the category of research-oriented sources, in the initial stages of their research students found books and review articles helpful, as they provided an overview of the whole field and helped them to identify main themes and debates. However, as their research progressed books became less helpful because they contained old information. Theses were also an important source of relevant information and they provided students with examples of what is expected in a finished (and successful) thesis. Reading the literature review in theses also helped students to understand different approaches to writing up their literature reviews and the importance of critical thinking. Students appreciated the importance of refereed journal articles, which tended to dominate their literature reviews. As their research progressed, students found conference papers to be important sources of current information and thinking. However, it is worth noting that individual disciplines and fields have their own patterns of publishing, so although conference papers may be considered extremely important in some disciplines, e.g. engineering, they may be less important as information sources for students in other disciplines, e.g. education. The changing needs in this area are illustrated in the Figure 5.4.

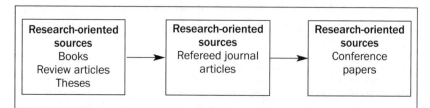

Figure 5.4 *Research students' use of different information sources*

The research community

An important information source for doctoral students is the research community, and Chu and Law (2006) identify three sources: students' supervisors, external experts and online discussion groups. There are differences in the importance of supervisors, which Chu and Law link to the original source of the research topic. For engineering students whose research is linked to grants achieved by their department or faculty, their supervisor's importance was related to the fact that she was likely to have written the bid for the grant, which was based on her area of specialism. She would thus be able to pass on knowledge of information sources to her doctoral students. Alternatively, the student might be carrying out research in an area where the supervisor hoped to develop her expertise and had already carried out preliminary work leading to some knowledge of relevant information sources. In contrast, Chu and Law found that education students tended to choose their own topics, which might be outside their supervisor's field of expertise. In addition, they found that students needed more support during the earlier rather than the later stages of their research. This is not surprising, as new doctoral students will still be exploring and learning about both their chosen subject and the associated information sources. An engineering student quoted by Chu and Law (2006, 34) stated:

My supervisor plays an essential role in my searching for certain important information. For example, he knows who the key researchers are in my field.

Figure 5.5 illustrates students' changing use of the research community.

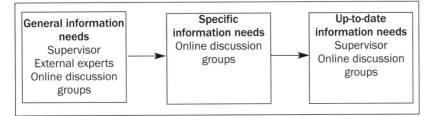

Figure 5.5 *Research students' use of the research community*

As the students travel along their research journeys, they begin to build up their knowledge and expertise, important contacts and information sources. As this process occurs they are likely to find their own voice in relation to their research, so that it becomes owned by them rather than by their supervisors. However, it is worth pointing out that although there appear to be differences in the level of contact between research students and their supervisors, and these are related to their disciplines (e.g. engineering students appear to have more contact with supervisors than do education students), to working practices within different departments, faculties and universities, and to individual styles in working on research and with a supervisor or student.

Research students also make use of external experts and, as with supervisors, these contacts are often more important in the early rather than the later stages of the research. Such experts may provide students with additional contacts or references. Another external source used by research students is online discussion groups (mailing lists and newsgroups). These are often international in make-up and provide students with access to a wide range of ideas and debate. Chu and Law found that such groups served three main purposes – sharing of ideas and opinions, troubleshooting and working groups on common issues or problems. The most common reason for using online discussion groups was to exchange ideas and opinions. Chu and Law (2006, 35) quote one education student:

> I mainly use two discussion groups. One is Sportpsy, which is mainly US and actually we can say it is universal. It has all kinds of members including professors and students who discuss issues in sports psychology. Another mailing list I use is the PE Talk Digest for teachers to discuss their ideas. For example, what to play during a class.

Chu and Law found that discussion groups for troubleshooting and working groups on common issues or problems were most commonly used by researchers engaged in technical research, e.g. engineering students

Other information sources

Research students use a range of other information sources, including bibliographic support services, professional literature, academic tool books, media and statistics. Use of these sources varies according to the discipline and, in the case of bibliographic support services, the experience of the student. Figure 5.6 provides a general overview of how research students may use these information sources.

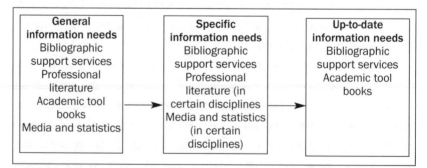

Figure 5.6 *Research students' use of other information sources*

Bibliographic support services were rated highly by research students who identified the importance of reference librarians and interlibrary loans. Chu and Law quote the experiences of an education student:

In the beginning, what I needed was easy to find and so the importance of reference librarians to me was low. Later on, I needed to dig deeper into my information search and certain information was hard to find; I got more help from reference librarians.

The importance of professional sources such as trade journals varies depending on the discipline of the researcher and on the stage of the research process. Some trade journals were found helpful by engineering students in the early stages of their research, as they provided easily accessible information. However, as their research progressed these sources became less important and the students turned to more scholarly sources. Some professional sources are very important for students, e.g. technical reports, standards and patents are important sources for engineering students, while government reports, educational standards and statistics are important for education students. The links between academic and professional communities vary according to discipline. Chu and Law describe the link as strong in engineering, where the professional communities produce outputs such as patents and reports that are of interest. In contrast, teachers apparently rarely have the time or energy to read academic journals, and so the links between academic research and practice are weaker.

Academic tool books are textbooks written for research students to help them learn about the research process and how to achieve their award. Examples include:

Bell, J. (1999) *Doing your Research project. A guide for first-time researchers in education and social science,* Open University.
Wellington, J., Bathmaker, A-M., Hunt, C., McCullock, G. and Sikes, P. (2005) *Succeeding with Your Doctorate*, Sage.
Wisker, G. (2001) *The Postgraduate Research Handbook*, Palgrave.

Chu and Law suggest that some students find these books most useful in the early stages of research but that once they have gained an understanding of it then they don't refer to them again. In contrast, they also found that some students rated these sources highly towards the end of the doctoral process, when they required advice on structuring and formatting their theses. They quote an education student:

> I mainly read the book 'How to get a PhD?' Why is it useful? Because while I am doing my PhD, certain doubts arise. For example, 'It is only me doing the research', 'Nobody knows what I am doing', 'I don't know whether my research is worth doing', or 'I don't know if I should continue my research'. Reading these kinds of books will help me deal with feelings like these . . . They help me tune in better. I have found that they are becoming more and more useful.
>
> (Chu and Law, 2006, 36)

My own experience was that, at each stage in the research process, I visited and revisited the relevant chapters in academic tool books such as Wellington et al. (2005). This helped me to understand each stage in detail and I found that the textbook, which contained many case studies, also provided reassurance and validation of my experiences.

Other sources used by students include newspapers, government publications and statistical sources. The value of these different sources depends on the discipline and the topic of research.

What are the implications of Chu and Law's research on doctoral students' information needs for the providers of library and information services and support? It appears to indicate that students' information needs are complex and that they vary according to the students' prior information experiences, their stage of research and their discipline. This suggests that library and information staff need to engage with these students during their research so as to help them to identify and use different information sources at different stages in their projects. This topic is explored in more depth in Chapter 6.

Summary

This chapter has provided an overview of research skills training programmes for doctoral students and an indication of the wide range of study-related activities a research student may be involved in. It has also provided an example of the library and information skills training offered as a taught module within the research skills training programme. The chapter included a case study in which the information needs of doctoral students at different stages in their research journeys were outlined and discussed with reference to their progress along that path.

6

Supporting research students in academic libraries and information services

Introduction

Many academic library and information workers are involved in supporting research students. This chapter explores different approaches to supporting research students, including induction, workshops, one-to-one support and electronic support. Approaches to targeting and communicating with research students are also considered. Towards the end of this chapter, a self-assessment inventory is provided which will enable you to identify your approaches to supporting research students. It will be a tool for reflection and for the identification of potential areas of development as well as areas of good practice which might be shared across the information services sector.

The information presented in this chapter is based on research into current practice through visits (physical and virtual) to a range of academic libraries, and also informal discussions with colleagues who have attended my workshops on 'Supporting Research Students' at CILIP. The range of support offered to research students varies, depending on the type of university, the focus of the library and information services, the numbers of research students and the development plans of the institution. Many institutions are now focusing on developing and expanding their research activities and increasing their numbers of research students. For these institutions, enhancing the support available to research students is high on their agenda.

While the levels and types of support for taught students appear to be fairly similar across different universities, it soon became apparent to me that there is much less uniformity in terms of provision of support for research students. The self-assessment inventory at the end of this chapter brings together all the different ways in which library and information workers are supporting research students. As this is a constantly developing field, the different ways in which these students are supported will continue to grow and develop.

Information needs

Barry (1997) argues that research students have the greatest information needs and therefore, of all students, the greatest need for information skills. She suggests that their information needs are even greater than those of established academics, as they need to provide comprehensive and up-to-date literature reviews in their theses. In addition, 'postgraduate researchers have not yet built up the same information reserves as more established academics: rich personal collections of publications and a network of personal contact with expert colleagues, which can short cut the need for extensive information-seeking and thus employment of information skills' (Barry, 1997, 229).

As outlined in Chapter 5, research students require access to a wide range of information resources including textbooks and monographs, electronic journals, databases, reports (e.g. from project websites), conference papers and online discussion boards. They also need access to different types of resources at different stages in their research. Some research students will start their PhD programme with experience of using a basic range of information sources, e.g. textbooks and a few journals (printed or electronic), plus searching the internet using fairly basic search strategies. In order to be successful in their research, they need to develop advanced information skills and this learning process typically takes place during the early stages of research, while they are producing their literature reviews. Library and information workers provide vital support to research students throughout their research. In this chapter, I outline different approaches to supporting students throughout the learning and research processes.

Current approaches to supporting research students

Library and information services currently support research students by a variety of means, including:

- generic induction sessions that provide an overview of services and resources
- specific training sessions
- provision of taught credit-bearing and non-credit-bearing modules and units on information skills
- support from a named member of staff or team with special responsibility for research students
- specialist online resources and services
- virtual graduate schools (see Chapter 7).

These categories form the structure for the next few sections of this chapter.

Induction sessions

In some academic libraries and information services, induction for research students may be the only structured opportunity that the staff have for meeting with these students. However, as discussed in Chapter 1, some students will be experiencing culture shock, and maybe also learning shock, at the time when induction is normally scheduled, making it difficult for them to benefit fully from the session. In addition, library induction sessions are often sandwiched within a whole series of formal presentations, resulting in students soon experiencing information overload. This means that they are less likely to learn from the session. The audience at general induction sessions is likely to be very broad, ranging from students with limited experience of academic libraries and information services through to those with advanced information skills. Thus, although formal induction sessions offer a welcome opportunity to meet new students, they perhaps provide an occasion that is limited to raising the students' awareness of services and resources.

Unlike students on taught undergraduate and postgraduate programmes, who start their programmes at a fixed time in the academic year, e.g. September or January, research students are sometimes permitted to enrol at any time of the year. If this is the case, it will mean that they miss out on scheduled induction events aimed at a whole cohort of new research students. For many of these students, this may mean that their induction is limited and dependent on their department or faculty, who may not involve the library and its staff.

Informal discussions with colleagues in a range of academic library and information services indicate that they may be involved in the following types of activities aimed at students starting their research:

- sending letters to new research students to welcome them to the university and provide general information about the library and information service and contact details
- providing leaflets and guidebooks which focus on the likely requirements of new research students
- providing a pre-induction and/or induction website which gives research students general information about library and information services and access to information about training programmes, specialist links and information resources; some of these websites include podcasts or video clips that present the

experiences of research students; these 'talking heads' appear to provide reassurance and useful information to new students
- presentations made as part of an induction event, providing general information about library services and resources
- library tours.

In addition, some library and information workers attend social and other events organized at the start of the academic year as a means of making contact with and getting to know the research students.

Specific training sessions

Many library and information services provide a range of specific training sessions or workshops. These may be targeted at different groups of researchers, such as: all postgraduate students; only students enrolled on research degrees; or research staff and students. They are likely to be advertised via the library website, newsletters, graduate schools or direct e-mails to research students. These training sessions may last from one or two hours up to six hours. Typically, they involve a mixture of learning and teaching activities, including presentations, hands-on activities and use of quizzes and inventories, and the workshops may be supported by workbooks, training guides and e-learning.

Popular topics for workshops targeted at research students include:

- academic writing skills
- citation indexing and tools
- conference papers
- copyright
- electronic journals
- getting published
- grey literature
- guidance on referencing

- keeping up to date
- reference management tools
- specialist databases and indexes
- statistics and other data
- theses and dissertations
- using special collections and other materials.

A sample session plan for a one-hour workshop on referencing, aimed at research students in business and management, is outlined in Case Study 6.1. The session plan (see Table 6.1) indicates that the trainer intends using a range of learning and teaching activities, with a clear focus on the students being active during the workshop. It also shows how the different activities are linked to the learning outcomes.

Case Study 6.1: Example session plan – introduction to referencing

Aim
The aim of this session is to introduce business school research students to the standards of referencing expected in a doctoral thesis.

Learning outcome
As a result of attending this workshop, research students will be able to:

1 Use the Harvard method to correctly reference resources used in their doctoral thesis
2 Reference a range of resources, including books, journals, company reports and websites
3 Produce a list of the references in their thesis.

Table 6.1 *Example session plan*

Approximate timings	Indicative programme	Learning and teaching activities	Link to learning outcomes
5 minutes	Introduction and learning outcomes	Trainer introduces session and outlines learning outcomes	
5 minutes	Reasons for referencing	Small group activity with feedback	
10 minutes	Introduction to Harvard method	Presentation	1
10 minutes	Right and wrong methods of referencing	Worksheet activity in pairs	1
10 minutes	Referencing different resources	Pair activity. Students present their findings to whole group	2
5 minutes	Producing a list of references	Mini presentation	3
10 minutes	Summary	'Right and wrong' activity	1, 2, 3
2 minutes	Advertise EndNote™ workshop	Mini presentation	
3 minutes	Close	Mini presentation	

Taught modules on library and information research skills

Many library and information services provide taught modules on library and information research skills. These modules (or units) may be credit bearing, i.e. successful completion of the module enables the student to gain academic credit, which counts towards an academic award, or they may be non-credit bearing. An example of a credit-bearing module is provided in Chapter 5.

Case Study 6.2 is an example of a programme provided for research students. This is an extensive case study and has some interesting features, including the following:

- Students are provided with a programme of workshops over a six-week period.
- The programme is supported by e-learning, i.e. it is a blended learning programme.
- The programme is delivered by team teaching.
- The tutors, who were studying for Postgraduate Certificates in Higher Education (PGCHE), used the design and implementation of the programme as an activity that contributed to their awards.

Case Study 6.2: MI512 research training course for PhD students

This case study describes a research training course provided for PhD students by library staff working in collaboration with the Centre for Learning Technology at the London School of Economics (LSE). MI512: Information Literacy, Tools for Research, is a non-credit-bearing course for PhD students and MSc Social Research students and the programme outline is influenced by the SCONUL Seven Pillars of Information Literacy (SCONUL, 2006). The programme tutors were students for the Postgraduate Certificate in Education, which provided them with formal opportunities to reflect on their work.

The programme
MI512 is a six-week programme of two-hour workshops supported by a virtual learning environment based on Moodle. It includes:

Week 1: Introduction to literature searching: Finding books and journals, using Cross Searcher (LSE's federated search), IBSS and ISI citation indexes, finding materials not stocked at LSE.
Week 2: Going beyond Google: Quality issues, using Google Advanced Search, using Google Scholar and Google Books, iGoogle, other search engines, using Intute and Delicious™.
Week 3: Finding newspapers, theses, conference papers: Using Nexis,

using the Index to Theses/Ethos, using ZETOC, what are pre-prints?, and finding research publications, including LSE Research Online.

Week 4: Citing and referencing for your thesis: Introduction to the Harvard method, managing your references, citing books, journals and web pages, using Delicious™ to store web references.

Week 5: Using EndNote™: Introduction to EndNote™, adding records manually, importing records from the Library Catalogue and from IBSS, producing a simple bibliography, selecting and applying a range of bibliographic styles.

Week 6: Keeping up to date and next steps: Setting up e-mail alerts, citation searching in ISI, introduction to RSS, using Google Reader to read feeds, social networks and e-mail lists. Getting help in the future.

Learning and teaching activities

The learning and teaching sessions were structured to include short presentations and demonstrations from tutors, leaving more time for hands-on work. Tutors aimed to talk for no more than 15 minutes before allowing hands-on practice. Activities were grouped so that students had longer hands-on sessions, rather than illustrating each activity separately and then allowing only a few minutes for each activity. This enabled the more advanced students to skip those exercises with which they were familiar and to concentrate on the parts that were new to them. Grouping the hands-on exercises together in longer segments also enabled the tutors to spend longer on roving help.

Tutors provided the students with a workbook that included activities, hints and tips, reasons why the featured databases and resources are useful, further exercises and suggestions for those more advanced or already familiar with the featured databases, screen shots and clear instructions. They also included a pre-course assessment and a post-course assessment form.

A virtual learning environment based on Moodle provided additional support and was integrated into the classroom activities, with interactive tasks and quick access links. Students retained access to Moodle after the end of the course. The Moodle site was also used to deliver news and reminders via the News forum and each week also included its own topic forum.

Assessment

The pre-course assessment activity asked students to provide information about their research topics. It also asked for details of any prior library training and the online databases with which students were familiar. Students were asked to rate their confidence in finding literature and in searching the internet on a scale of 1 to 5. This assessment was repeated on completion of the course as a means of identifying progress.

Student confidence before attending the programme
   Finding published literature: 2.9
   Searching the internet: 2.85
Student confidence after attending the programme
   Finding published literature: 4.5
   Searching the internet: 4.3

Students completed details of their research topics, enabling tutors to have a better idea of the subjects represented. The tutors also gave students feedback, indicating the best databases to search for their subjects (and how they could be accessed), useful websites and other libraries, and advice on search strategies. This feedback demonstrated the value of the class to students early on, and helped them establish a rapport with the tutors. It also helped the tutors to deal with mixed-ability and mixed-subject groups, enabling them to give more tailored advice during the hands-on exercises.

Team tutoring

MI512 is team-taught by two lead tutors, with additional assistance from two colleagues. Team teaching allowed the tutors to build up a rapport so that they could support each other. It also allowed for more variation in class, and enabled tutors to provide roving help to students during the hands-on sessions. This is particularly helpful when dealing with mixed-ability groups as trainers can encourage students working at different levels during the hands-on exercises. It is also useful to have multiple trainers so as to provide cover during sickness/absence etc., and to have an extra person in the room to help with checking in attendees (particularly useful with larger groups). The students clearly appreciated having the same trainers throughout the term so as to build up rapport. They also occasionally called upon the trainers' expertise outside the classroom, suggesting the course is more suitably given by experienced library trainers.

Building learning relationships

Running a six-week course helped the tutors to develop a rapport with the students. Even something as simple as knowing who the students are and their names makes a big difference, as students can see that the tutors take an interest in them. It also gives tutors more confidence to adopt a relaxed manner, to use students' names and refer to their research projects in class. This is difficult to achieve in stand-alone classes.

Progressive learning is more beneficial to the students because they build skills and confidence week on week, and develop rapport with their tutors to a degree not possible in a one-off class. The library training has more impact on students and they can develop their skills to a greater degree. Being able to use their own examples in exercises is very important. This is harder to achieve in stand-alone classes, as tutors prepare more generic searches, not being aware of students' research topics. Feedback from students suggested they were happy to attend a programme of classes and many commented that they set aside the time each week to build up their skills.

Student feedback

Feedback from students was excellent as indicated by the following sample comments:

> The overall course was excellent, You have raised the bar very high!
> *1st year, Geography and Environment*

I liked that this was a 6-week course and you could build up your information literacy . . . I liked the pre-course needs analysis form and individual suggestions for search sources.
2nd year, Social Policy

Without exaggeration, this is the most well prepared, organized and professional course I've ever experienced in my life. The pre-class organization is impressive, the Moodle resources outstanding, the hand-outs just right, the co-teaching smooth and collegial, the follow-up effective. I will keep this course in mind as a model for when I prepare my own course in the future.
1st year, Government

Key benefits of the course

Benefits of the course included:

- Students were provided with an introduction to literature searching and taken through a variety of resources to help them find, manage and evaluate the resources they would use while writing a thesis.
- Many students commented that the course was a good investment of time, as it saved them time in the long run and helped to ensure they were using appropriate sources and databases for their research. Concerns that they had been 'missing something' from the literature were very common and MI512 gave them the skills to know where to search.
- Students were given specific feedback on useful resources, search strategies and other useful libraries for their thesis topics, using feedback forms which would be valuable throughout their time as researchers.
- Students were put in contact with their liaison librarians so they could receive ongoing support during their research.
- All class activities focused on the students' own topics, so they built up research skills and found useful information in a safe learning environment. Each week they left the classroom having discovered new useful resources and articles and they could very quickly see the practical benefits of the course.

- Students were able to meet other research students from across the school, and work together to help each other and share ideas. Isolation is a particular problem for PhD students, who may struggle to meet other researchers outside their department.
- Tutors were on hand to offer advice and help in class; and after the class, students had someone to contact if they ran into problems.
- Although the course was aimed at students starting an extensive literature search, others at different stages of their research attended and commented that they found it useful.

General benefits for information skills training at LSE

Work on the MI512 programme has had a number of other benefits for library training more generally. These include:

- All the positives learned from MI512 and taking the PGCHE are being rolled out to general information skills training courses.
- MI512 illustrated the use of Moodle in classes and the importance of developing a blended learning approach to training.
- Staff identified the potential for rolling out MI512 to departments within the LSE.
- The programme provided an excellent example of collaboration between Centre for Learning Technology and library staff.
- Team teaching allowed tutors to benefit from the skills and expertise of colleagues and to develop their own approaches.
- MI512 course materials have been adapted for use on other information skills training courses.

Relevance of MI512 to the wider library and information community

- Whilst many universities offer training workshops and online support to research students, MI512 seems to be unique in that it is the only long-term, overall programme of research workshops, as opposed to stand-alone classes or one-day events.
- The work was presented at an international conference, LILAC (Librarians' Information Literacy Annual Conference[1]) in 2009, and

many librarians in other institutions requested guest access to the Moodle course. The success of the programme has received widespread recognition in the library profession and the tutors are considering further dissemination and publication.

Reference
SCONUL (Society of College, National and University Libraries) (2006) *The Seven Pillars of Information Literacy*. Available at: www.sconul.ac.uk/ groups/information_literacy/sp/seven_pillars.html.

Acknowledgement
This case study is provided with the kind permission of Rowena Macrae-Gibson, Liaison Librarian, LSE Library and Dr Jane Secker, Learning Technology Librarian, Centre for Learning Technology, LSE.

Support from a named individual member of staff or a specialist team

It is common practice for a professional librarian or information worker to be a named liaison person for a department or unit, and his brief may extend to supporting research students. In addition, there may be a team of specialist librarians supporting specific research centres, departments or groups of research students. The type of support provided by the liaison or specialist subject librarians to research students is likely to vary but may include the following:

- individual advice and guidance on all aspects of information literacy via face-to-face meetings, e-mail, telephone, Skype™ communication, text messages or instant messaging
- specialist workshops and training sessions
- advice and help sheets on a range of topics, e.g. using specific databases
- drop-in help sessions

- specialist online resources and advice, e.g. via a website, virtual learning environment or portal
- up-to-date news and information via a weblog, e-bulletins or other resources
- attendance and support at staff/student committees
- attendance and support at departmental and faculty research committees.

A colleague at a post-1992 university made the following comment:

> We are still developing our research activities and have a small number of research students (12) in the science faculty. I make an appointment to meet each new PhD student when they arrive and talk them through how I can help them. Every other Wednesday afternoon I provide a drop-in help session for an hour in a small computing lab. Normally 3-4 PhD students turn up. They ask me for help with literature searching and on topics such as RefWorks™. I found that they wanted help with SPSS™, I can't help with that so I got a friend from the computing department to come and help them. I've got to know all the PhD students and have a friendly relationship with them. I don't know how long I'll be able to run this type of personal service – once numbers of PhD students increase, then it will be difficult.

Specialist online resources and services

Library and information services provide a range of online resources and services for researchers, including research students. Webb, Gannon-Leary and Bent (2007) provide a useful overview of surveys into researchers' experiences and information needs. From the perspectives of researchers, one of the most important services provided by libraries is access to electronic journals, followed by a comprehensive collection which includes specialist materials, archives and special collections. Another important service is the document delivery service.

Many university library and information services provide specialist web pages and support for researchers, which typically provide introductory and contact information, world of research, information skills, accessing other libraries, writing and publishing, plagiarism and referencing, and online training courses. The following lists provide examples of the typical contents of the research pages of the websites of academic libraries:

Introductory information

- Staff information
- Service information
- Frequently asked questions (FAQs)

World of research

- Information on grants and bidding for funding
- Access to external tools and resources such as Mendeley (www.mendeley.com, an academic networking site that enables individual researchers to manage their own research resources and share them with others)
- Access to research networks
- Intellectual property
- Knowledge exchange

Information skills

- Finding and accessing electronic journals
- Finding and accessing databases and indexes
- Finding and accessing statistics and other data
- Finding and accessing theses and dissertations
- Finding and accessing conference papers
- Finding and accessing grey resources

- Information and access information on special collections and other materials
- Access to a repository of research material produced at the university, e.g. peer reviewed journal articles, working papers, conference papers, technical reports and theses
- Keeping up to date

Accessing other libraries

- Information and guidance on access to other academic and specialist libraries, e.g. British Library
- Accessing and using other libraries catalogues

Writing and publishing

- Academic writing skills
- Open access publishing and archiving
- Getting published
- Copyright

Plagiarism and referencing

- Guidance on referencing
- Reference management tools

Online training courses (see also later in this chapter)

- Online training materials produced in-house
- Access to IT training courses provided within the university
- Access to external online training materials and programmes.

Many library websites provide guidance on keeping up to date and using RSS feeds that enable researchers to keep abreast of new items in online bibliographic databases, publishers' sites, news sites etc.

This may include a RSS feed to the library online research services. This guidance and the text-based resources may be augmented by interactive elements such as online reference help desks, weblogs, podcasts, discussion groups, etc. The development of social networking sites such as Facebook™ and information sharing sites such as Delicious™ provides new opportunities for libraries and information services to collect and share information and ideas.

Targeted support

So far this section has focused on generic online support services for researchers. Increasingly, universities are also providing targeted support for their research students. This tends to replicate the generic services and support for researchers, as outlined above.

The London School of Economics, for example, provides an online library companion for researchers via its virtual learning environment, and this provides access to help and resources on topics such as:

■ getting the best out of online searches
■ finding newspapers, conference papers and theses
■ finding government and intergovernmental organization (IGO) materials
■ keeping up-to-date with research
■ tracking key papers via citation searching
■ how to cite materials
■ using EndNote™
■ how to find material not in stock at LSE
■ sharing research
■ how to get help using LSE-provided software.

In addition, library and information online services are now commonly enhanced through the addition of Web 2.0 tools (see Chapter 7) such as:

- Flickr™
- RSS feeds
- podcasts
- Slideshare™
- social networking sites such as MySpace™, Facebook™, LinkedIn™
- Twitter™
- weblogs
- wikis
- videoclips or audiofiles.

Many library and information service websites also provide links to external sources of guidance for research students such as:

- Beyond the PhD (www.beyondthephd.co.uk), a career resource for arts and humanities PhD researchers which provides an interesting set of videos, audio clips and articles. It was shortlisted for the 2009 Times Higher Education ICT Initiative of the Year Award.
- Intute, available at www.intute.ac.uk, which provides advice and guidance to all students on finding and using credible information sources. This is an impressive resource and provides guidance, advice and tutorials for all students, and also for staff.
- Social Science Research Network (www.ssrn.com), which provides access to a range of specialist groups, e.g. economics, health and leadership, and supports sharing of research and resources.

Online courses

Many university library and information services provide access to a range of online courses from their websites. These may cover topics such as:

- academic writing skills, including publishing
- computer skills, e.g. basic IT skills; using MS Office™; using

Endnote™; using MS Project™; creating web pages/sites; they may also provide access to external courses such as those offered by companies such as Microsoft™
- general web skills and information skills using either internally produced courses or via access to external courses such as TONIC (The Online Netskills Interactive Course, supplied by Netskills, University of Newcastle); net.TUTOR (provided by the Ohio State University Libraries), which offers guidance on evaluating websites for research purposes; Internet Detective (supplied by Intute), another practical tutorial
- specialist databases and information resources, e.g. how to use Web of Knowledge
- specialist information skills training programmes, e.g. aimed at a specific discipline or field of research
- reference management courses e.g. on EndNote™ or RefWorks™.

Some university libraries provide specialist support and guidance for distance learners. For example, the University of Leicester provides the following guidance for distance learners and part-time research students:

- Accessing electronic resources off-campus
- Access to journal articles
- Access to library books
- Access to theses and dissertations
- Access to other libraries
- Distance learning service forms and guides
- Enquiry service, contact details, office hours and your feedback
- Improving your information and research skills
- Literature searches
- Managing your references and using RefWorks™ for citing references
- Registering for membership with the university library
- Resources

- Study and research days, residential and summer schools
- Using the library catalogue to find books and journals
- Visiting the university library.

A number of university library websites provide access to online courses. For example, Imperial College London has created a number of online modules, called Programmes of Information Literacy (PILS), which are available to all PhD students. These courses are delivered via the virtual learning environment Blackboard, and PILS aims to assist research students in:

- developing advanced research skills, including effective search techniques
- highlighting key resources to assist in your literature review and research
- examining how copyright and IP affect your work
- providing information on plagiarism
- giving advice on the publishing process, with a particular emphasis on open-access using Web 2.0 technologies to keep abreast of current awareness services, and research activities in your field.   (Imperial College[2])

Targeting and communicating with research students

An important issue for library and information workers who support research students is how to target research students and communicate with them. Informal discussions with librarians from a wide range of libraries indicate that this area is sometimes problematic. For example, some librarians reported that they found it difficult to obtain information such as names and e-mail addresses of research students from faculties and departments or from the graduate school. Other librarians reported that it was particularly difficult to identify and make contact with research students, and especially part-time students who started their research programmes at different times of the year. However, colleagues did report a wide range of strategies that they used to target research students. These are listed here:

Pre-induction

■ Distributing welcome letters, general information and contact details to research students in the welcome and registration packs sent out before they start their programmes
■ Providing leaflets and guidebooks which focus on the likely requirements of new research students
■ Providing pre-induction websites with welcome and general information (these websites sometimes contain audio or video clips of research students talking about their experiences)
■ Providing pre-induction and/or induction websites that offer research students general information about library and information services and access to information on training programmes, specialist links and information resources. Some websites also include podcasts or video clips which present the experiences of research students. These 'talking heads' help to provide reassurance and useful information to new students.

Induction

■ Presentations made as part of an induction event and providing general information about library services and resources
■ Leaflets and guidebooks
■ Library tours.

Throughout the academic year

■ E-mails and bulletins inviting students to workshops, training programmes or drop-in help sessions
■ E-mails and bulletins to supervisors advising them of the help

and support library staff can provide to research students

■ Online support and updating services using tools such as:
— RSS news channels
— weblogs
— links to student Facebook™ sites
— instant messaging and Twitter™
■ Posters inviting students to workshops, training programmes or drop-in help sessions. These posters are often strategically placed, e.g. in the library, faculties and departments, graduate school, international office, students' union
■ Regular help desks in faculties, student café and graduate school
■ Attendance by library staff at student social events
■ Attendance by library staff at staff/student committees, research committees and also research seminars
■ Internal funding to library staff for research projects and development activities which involve collaborative working with research students and academics
■ Involvement in graduate school activities, including delivery of taught modules and workshops aimed at research students and training events aimed at supervisors.

Self-assessment: how do you support research students?

Table 6.2 is a self-assessment inventory to enable you and your colleagues to identify ways in which you support research students. There are gaps in the table for you to add other approaches that are not included. When you have completed the table you may want to reflect on the findings and identify areas for development, and also areas of good practice that you wish to share across the library and information sector.

Table 6.2 *Self-assessment inventory*

Activity	Do you offer this service or support activity to research students?
Pre-induction and induction activities	
Sending letters to new research students	
Providing leaflets and guidebooks	
Providing a pre-induction and/or induction website	
Presentations during induction week	
Library tours	
Involvement in induction social and networking events	
Specific training sessions (typical topics)	
Academic writing skills	
Citation indexing and tools	
Conference papers	
Copyright	
Electronic journals	
Getting published	
Grey literature	
Guidance on referencing	
Keeping up to date	
Reference management tools	
Specialist databases and indexes	
Statistics and other data	
Theses and dissertations	
Using special collections and other materials	

Table 6.2 *Continued*	
Taught credit-bearing and non-credit bearing modules and units on information skills	
Credit- bearing module(s) or unit(s) (add titles)	
Non-credit-bearing module(s) or unit(s) (add titles)	
Support from a named member of staff or team	
Individual advice and guidance via face-to-face meetings, e-mail, telephone or online tools	
Specialist workshops and training sessions	
Advice and help sheets on a range of tools and resources	
Drop-in help sessions	
Specialist online resources and advice, e.g. via a website, virtual learning environment or portal	·
Up-to-date news and information via a weblog, e-bulletins or other resources	
Attendance and support at staff/student committees	
Attendance and support at departmental and faculty research committees	
Specialist online resources and services	
Introductory information	
Staff information	
Service information	
Frequently asked questions (FAQs)	
World of research	
Information on grants and bidding for funding	

Table 6.2 *Continued*	
Access to external tools and resources	
Access to research networks	
Intellectual property	
Knowledge exchange	
Information skills	
Finding and accessing electronic journals	
Finding and accessing databases and indexes	
Finding and accessing statistics and other data	
Finding and accessing theses and dissertations	
Finding and accessing conference papers	
Finding and accessing grey resources	
Information and access information on special collections and other materials	
Access to a university repository	
Keeping up to date	
Accessing other libraries	
Information and guidance on access to other academic and specialist libraries	
Accessing and using other libraries' catalogues	
Writing and publishing	
Academic writing skills	
Open access publishing and archiving	
Getting published	
Copyright	
Plagiarism and referencing	
Guidance on referencing	
Reference management tools	
Online training courses	
Computer skills	
General web skills and information skills	
Specialist databases and information resources	
Specialist information skills training programmes	

Table 6.2 *Continued*	
Reference management courses, e.g. on EndNote™ or RefWorks™	
Other services and support activities	

Summary

This chapter has explored different approaches to supporting research students, including induction, workshops, one-to-one support and electronic support. It has provided guidance on common practices that libraries and information services have developed for supporting research students. It has also looked at ways of targeting and communicating with research students. The self-assessment inventory at the end of the chapter will enable readers to identify their own approaches to supporting research students, and will provide a tool for reflection and the identification of potential areas of development, as well as areas of good practice that might be shared across the sector.

Notes

1 www.lilacconference.com/.
2 http://www3.imperial.ac.uk/library/learningandsupport/teaching/ students.

7

Virtual graduate schools

Introduction

The aim of this chapter is to present and explore the idea of supporting research students in a virtual graduate school (VGS). The concept of a VGS is an online environment where research students can come together to access a range of resources, to meet and discuss common issues with each other and perhaps with their supervisors. Different approaches to developing a VGS are explored in some depth.

The development of virtual graduate schools

The concept of a VGS has developed as a result of a number of drivers, including:

- the need to support research students and encourage them to complete their degrees
- the need to provide students with access to a community where they can make friends, share ideas and learn from each other
- recognition that there may be research students in different faculties and departments who are grappling with the same methodological issues as their peers in other parts of the university and who welcome the opportunity to share their experiences and ideas

- the benefits of capturing and sharing the experiences of researchers (including students, contract staff and academics)
- the need to support and provide flexible research skills training
- the availability of virtual learning environments
- the availability of online tools, including Web 2.0 social networking and other tools.

Behind the development of a VGS there is often recognition that the research student experience is a very individual one and that some students may work in isolation and find it difficult to become part of a research community. This may be because there are small numbers of research students in their department or faculty, they may be distance research students, or they may be working away from their campus, e.g. doing fieldwork. The idea of developing a virtual community with access to discussion groups is an attractive one, as it suggests the possibility of developing online communities of research students and staff. Also, research students in different departments or faculties may be working on the same methodological issues, e.g. research students in education and in management may be using an action research approach to their work, or students in gender studies and leadership may be using discourse analysis. The idea of enabling students from different departments and faculties to work together is attractive, as it suggests that students may learn from each other by sharing resources and ideas.

Individual researchers complete their doctoral theses, which then become available via the university's library or repository, and they may publish their findings in academic and professional journals. However, during the writing up process much of the 'messiness' of the research process is lost and emotional elements of a student's research experience may be edited out. Research students may thus obtain a distorted perception of the research process by reading textbooks and journal articles. Informal discussions with PhD students indicate that they enjoy hearing the 'stories' of research activities from other students and from more experienced researchers. These stories may be captured in text, audio or video recordings and presented within a VGS as a means of both capturing and sharing individual research experiences.

Another benefit of developing a VGS is that it can support and provide flexible research skills training, e.g. through the availability of online courses and by providing training materials and other resources. Examples of online courses and training resources are outlined in Chapter 6.

Virtual learning environments (VLEs) are extensively used in higher education. The development of sites for research communities and to enhance the experiences of doctoral students is a logical progression. While VLEs are often structured around the modules or units and administrative needs of taught students, they do provide a space with potential for the development of a community of research students and for enhancing their experience.

Typically, VLEs provide tools such as announcements, discussion boards, file handling, web links, e-mail, drop-boxes and survey tools. The availability of online tools, including social networking tools, provides an attractive means of supporting and engaging with research students. Commonly used tools include:

- *Audio podcasts*, which enable members to listen to recordings using an MP3 player. For example, the recording may be of a particular aspect of a researcher's experience or a particular stage in the PhD journey, e.g. the *viva* examination.
- *Blogs or weblogs*, which enable individual students, researchers and others, e.g. liaison librarians and other information specialists, to post news and useful links or to reflect on their own experiences. Some VGSs enable members to host their own blogs, while others limit blogs to individuals who are managing the site or contributing to it, e.g. liaison librarians or information workers.
- *RSS* (Really Simple Syndication or Rich Site Summary), which enables individuals to gain updates or web feeds from other

websites as they are updated. This means that an individual
researcher can be alerted to new blog entries, news headlines,
new journal articles on a specific topic and new audio or video
clips. A VGS may provide RSS feeds for its members.

■ *Twitter*™, the social networking and micro-blogging service that
enables individuals to send and receive extremely short text
messages, known as 'tweets', which can be up to 140 characters
long. Tweets can be sent via the Twitter™ website, by SMS
(short messaging service) or through other applications.

■ *Videos*, which provide a means of sharing the experience and
expertise of doctoral students and researchers in the VGS.

■ *Wikis*, which enable different users to contribute to and edit the
same web page. The commonest example of a wiki is Wikipedia.
Wikis may be provided to enable members to develop joint
materials and resources together.

Case Study 7.1: University of Hull Virtual Graduate School and the Graduate Virtual Research Environment

Stage 1: The Hull University Business School Virtual Graduate School (adapted from Loureiro-Koechlin, 2008)

In January 2008 Hull University Business School began a project called the
Virtual Graduate School (HUBS VGS), supported by Roberts Funding
(funding provided by the UK government for the development of
professional and personal skills for doctoral students following the
publication of the Roberts Report, described in Chapter 5). The aim of the
HUBS VGS is to provide students with an accessible learning resource that
they can return to as often as needed during their research journeys. In
particular, the virtual resource facilitates knowledge transfer from
successful students and researchers to those with less experience.
Knowledge gained during the PhD journey is often disseminated across a
narrow subject field, and much of the 'messiness' and complexity involved
in the research process is lost during writing up for publication. The HUBS

VGS contains multi-media resources (podcasts, videoclips, PowerPoint™ presentations) contributed by current and former PhD students and academic staff, showing students what to expect during the PhD experience. All resources are grounded in the experiences of PhD students and early career researchers and are presented in a blogger tool, enabling all members to discuss and share their experiences.

Features

The HUBS VGS has the following features:

- general and subject-specific resources on research skills and career development
- reusable resources
- discussion boards focused on specific research issues (online focus groups or communities based on common interests)
- knowledge transfer from experienced to less experienced researchers
- access to additional resources, e.g. selected books and journal articles.

The development of the site involved the project worker in collecting information from two focus groups with students and academic staff in the Business School. This information provided very useful insights into what was needed to help students and staff learn and carry out research. The outcomes of these focus groups are presented in Figure 7.1 (overleaf).

Starting from the right hand side of the diagram, focus group participants stated that essential support was needed to provide them with information about the requirements that they must meet in order to complete their research. This information will complement material about the actual research process at all its stages. On the left hand side, students and staff expressed their desire to develop the current Business School research communities.

Suggestions included providing support to research centres, supporting groups of supervisors and allowing 'critical friends' to meet (online and then in real life). The concept of a critical friend arose in the focus group

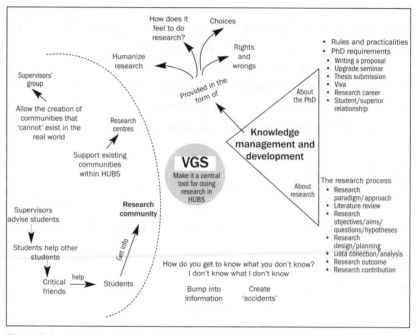

Figure 7.1 *Outcome of focus groups (Loureiro-Koechlin, 2008)*

meetings, and is someone, not necessarily a supervisor, who can provide a critical view on another person's research. Another suggestion to emerge was that an online environment can be a place where people can *bump into other people by accident*, and come to know useful information which otherwise they would not be able to access (bottom of diagram). Finally, one of the most important issues raised was the need for a human perspective on carrying out research. Students suggested that standard published information about research methodologies and requirements could be found in books and journal articles, but what they felt was missing in traditional research resources was an insight into the actual process of carrying out research. This means gaining insight into the experiences of researchers, e.g. their decisions, mistakes, challenges and the 'messiness' of the research process. These issues are often hidden aspects of research and may not be reflected in books or journal articles.

With the above information, the project team decided that the following would be important features of the HUBS VGS site:

- using individual research case studies; this means that the resources provided in the HUBS VGS are created by and belong to staff or students, and represent what they are actually doing
- using visual and audio media wherever possible, as this helps to capture important human and social issues involved in carrying out research
- using work-in-progress materials such as essay drafts, student notes and PowerPoint™ presentations, to provide a sense of how researchers come up with and develop ideas and how researchers progress in time until they complete their projects
- allowing users to create their own resources to share with the others
- including areas for HUBS VGS users to interact with each other, e.g. by commenting on the research resources provided or by conversing about different research-related topics.

With these features in mind, the project team began implementation of the HUBS VGS site using the university's VLE, eBridge.

Implementation

The implementation process involved two main activities:

1 *Creation of research resources*: The project team contacted students and staff who were willing to share their research. Most of them agreed to produce video and/or audio podcasts for the project. Other kinds of material (essays in Word, PowerPoint™ presentations) were used when participants did not feel comfortable with recording equipment or were not on campus. Video and audio podcasts last an average of seven minutes and focused on one or two aspects of research. Video taping was carried out in different places within the Business School, offices, seminar rooms, meeting rooms, etc. The locations were usually selected by the presenters.

2 *Customization of the eBridge environment*: The HUBS VGS uses one site within eBridge. Within this site three main tools are used:

- *Overview tool:* This is a tool that offers a *free text* space which is used to provide guidance on how to use the site.
- *Blogger:* This is a weblog tool which the team renamed 'Research Gallery' within the VGS site. Posts have been created as short articles, showing the actual resource (video, PowerPoint™ etc.), contextual information, references to books, journal articles, websites, questions to help the reader think about the topic discussed and a box suggesting related topics and links.
- *Forum tool:* Forums are areas that host discussion threads. Four forums were created: 'Research', 'Your degree', 'Being in touch' and 'About this website'. All HUBS VGS members are free to start and participate in any topic of conversation.

Evaluation

The project proved a success and accumulated 200 registered users in 12 months. Initial evaluation of the HUBS VGS indicated that it provides an additional and valued resource, in terms of both supporting individual research journeys and developing an online community. The following are examples of doctoral student feedback:

> As a PhD student, I find the wide range of resources available on the Virtual Graduate School very useful and informative. In particular, I frequently refer to the VGS to visit the tips and guidance for managing the research process, writing up the thesis and *viva* preparation.

> The videos are very informative. Excellent image, very good sound, that's wonderful. I think the links to additional references or related topics are crucial.

> I have found the VGS website invaluable. I was able to upload my own PhD experiences to share with the rest of the community. Also, I was able to access various sources of information about some PhD students' experiences and academic and social events. Looking at

other people's experiences has indeed developed and enhanced my research skills, and is still doing so.

Stage 2: Graduate Virtual Research Environment

Following the success of the HUBS VGS, additional funding was received in order to develop a Graduate Virtual Research Environment (GVRE), which was aimed at all research students and researchers in the university. Again, the project was funded by the Roberts Fund. The new GVRE (Figure 7.2) was designed to augment and enhance current research methods training across the university, and it provides students and researchers with an accessible research skills learning resource.

The GVRE provides a series of learning journeys or research pathways suited to the needs of different disciplines across the university. These are organized by department or by subject specialism within a department. Many of the resources developed in the HUBS VGS are available and appropriate for reuse in other discipline areas. The resources have been

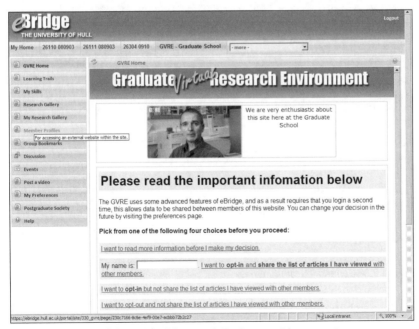

Figure 7.2 *The Graduate Virtual Research Environment home page*

enhanced by the addition of subtitles that helped capture main points as well as the language used by researchers. Individual tutors delivering research training can use the GVRE within their own modules and add to the research learning repository. The GVRE can thus be tailored to individual needs. That is, it can guide researchers in different areas through the pathway that they will take within their particular research projects, e.g. from project proposal to conference or journal article. The site was established with one main (generic) learning journey, using the competencies identified in the UK Research Councils' Joint Statement (2001). This is illustrated in Figure 7.3.

The learning resources are organized under the headings illustrated in Figure 7.2, providing another tool to help doctoral students develop their research skills. Guidance on information literacy is provided in section C.

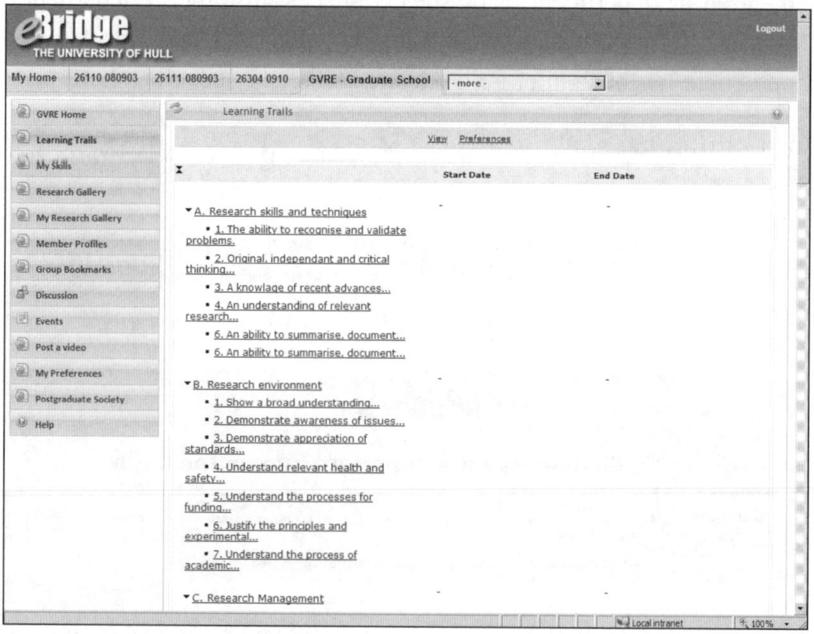

Figure 7.3 *Generic learning journey*

C. Research management
1 Apply effective project management by setting up research goals, intermediate milestones and prioritized of activities.

2 Design and execute systems for the acquisition and collation of information through the effective use of appropriate resources and equipment.

3 Identify and access appropriate bibliographical resources, archives, and other sources of relevant information.

4 Use information technology appropriately for database management, recording and presenting information.

Figure 7.4 provides an example of an entry in section C.3 which was developed by colleagues in academic services and aims to help research students find theses online.

In addition, the GVRE provides students with access to help in managing the development of their skills. Figure 7.5 (overleaf) shows the home page for this part of the site, where interactive activity enables students to identify and prioritize their research skills and transferable skills development activities.

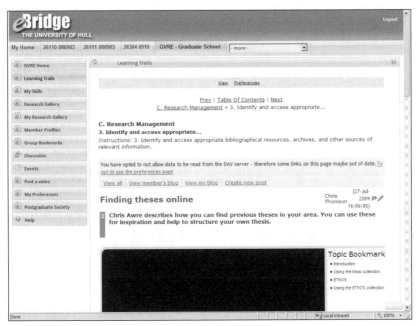

Figure 7.4 *Finding theses online*

Figure 7.5 *Skills development*

Unique features of the GVRE include:

- access to discipline-specific resources
- access to generic research resources
- access to support in developing transferable skills
- named research pathways to guide research students through the resources to meet the needs of specific disciplines
- knowledge transfer from successful researchers (postgraduate and postdoctoral researchers and new lecturers) via recorded interviews presented using podcasts or other Web 2.0 tools
- tracking devices to enable members to keep a record of their use of the GVRE (these also enable them to easily return to specific items)
- members may upload their own videos
- personal blog tools for members to create and maintain their own blogs
- personal wiki tools for members to create and engage with wikis
- access to other links e.g. University of Hull Postgraduate Society and Facebook™ site.

In order to promote use of the GVRE and to develop a community of interest among doctoral students and experienced researchers, it is actively marketed, e.g. at induction, and via other events and activities aimed at or organized by research students. In particular, the project team works with the Graduate School so that the GVRE is embedded in the taught modules provided as part of the research skills training.

Development processes of the HUBS VGS and GVRE

Development and implementation of the HUBS VGS and the GVRE took place over a two year period. Once the initial funding had been obtained from the university a steering group was established to oversee the HUBS VGS project. The group was chaired by the director of the Graduate School. Members included the pro-vice chancellor for learning and teaching, project workers and myself (as project leader). The group helped to establish the concept of a VGS and endorsed the direction of its development. It also supported crucial decisions regarding the development and implementation of the HUBS VGS and its subsequent transformation into the GVRE.

The development of the GVRE led to a new steering group, which was again headed by the director and included key staff from the Graduate School. This time, members included representatives from all faculties as well as the project team. In reality, it was difficult to obtain real engagement of members from across all faculties, but in time enthusiastic members did join the group.

A number of key decisions were endorsed by the steering groups. The first related to the production of learning resources. After considering the merits of either developing high quality video and audio resources or producing resources using fairly basic multimedia equipment, it was decided to produce 'rough and ready' videos and audio recordings. The reasoning for this was that students are familiar with the quality of resources available on websites such as YouTube™. Many students have equipment such as Flipvideo™ or mobile phones that allow quick and easy video recording which can then be uploaded to the HUBS VGS or the GVRE. Feedback from research students, e.g. at the focus group meetings and in one-to-one meetings, indicated that they welcomed this approach because it was 'friendly and accessible'. Individuals who were recorded said that they were quite comfortable with the process, as it was relaxed and informal. The final quality of video and audio clips produced using this approach was very good, with clear images and sound.

Another decision related to who should be recorded for the resources. The project team took a pragmatic approach and involved as many students and researchers as possible. The team wanted individuals at all stages in their research journeys and careers (from year one PhD students to professors) to be involved. This approach was successful and led to the development of a sense of community across both the HUBS VGS and the GVRE. However, all resources had to be checked to ensure that the comments of students and staff did not conflict with university regulations and procedures. In practice, the project team did not find that anything needed to be edited out of the recordings.

For the research narratives presented in the resources, the project worker asked doctoral students and academics to talk about particular aspects of their research journeys, e.g. literature searching, writing up, the viva. Some resources focus on the development of specific skills, e.g. project management, or the use of research tools such as NVivo™. This extensive case study provides an example of the development of the HUBS Virtual Graduate School and its successor the Graduate Virtual Research Environment, in which the focus was the development of a range of reusable learning resources through the involvement of students and staff across a university. The focus of these two projects included capturing the student experience so that their voices as well as those of more experienced researchers helped to shape the learning resources as well as the virtual graduate school.

Other approaches to developing a virtual graduate school

This section provides an example of the development of a virtual graduate school which takes a different approach. Banks, Wellington and Joyes (2008) write about the development of a VGS that involves capture of research narratives using video technology. Their project, the V-ResORT (Virtual Resources for Online Research Training) Project, was funded by the Higher Education Funding Council for England (HEFCE) through the Fund for the Development of Teaching and Learning (FDTL5) and was led by the University of Nottingham with the universities of Sheffield, Bath and Canterbury Christ Church. The V-ResORT Project developed innovative online learning materials that provide video narratives of researchers exploring key questions posed by the project team. The six main questions were:

1 Where did the ideas for research come from?
2 What is the aim and purpose of the research project?
3 Why were the theoretical and methodological approaches chosen?
4 How was your research project designed and conducted?
5 How was the research reported and communicated to a range of audiences?
6 What has happened to the research after it was completed?

The project team used MS Producer™ video streaming software to produce a series of 3–5 minute clips with PowerPoint™ slides, and also a transcript. The transcript helps students to work through the material and to develop their use of the language of research. In the evaluation of this work, Banks, Wellington and Joyes (2008) identify the value and importance of using video recordings of students as being that they resonate with the experiences of the students viewing them. They state:

> Reaction to the researcher narratives was positive and in some cases
> very enthusiastic, i.e. one student explained how having viewed one
> clip then found herself 'driven' to explore all twenty of the four minute
> clips to view the whole research story. She described how she listened
> to these at home whilst making and eating her evening meal. . . . the
> most popular video narrative for these Master's students was one by

an international PhD research student because they felt that her description of the challenges she had encountered was closest to their situation as beginning researchers.

Banks, Wellington and Joyes also identify the challenges that they experienced in this project. They comment on the importance of and the difficulties in embedding these materials as the starting point for developing online learning communities in professional doctorate programmes. They found that it was relatively easy to get students to engage with the production and use of video resources as an individual activity, but found it much more difficult to facilitate students working in collaborative groups. They suggest that this is because doctoral work is individual in nature, so students are working towards individual rather than collective goals. In other words, the nature of the doctoral process, with its emphasis on individualism, means that the full potential of a VGS is unfulfilled.

Implications for library and information workers

The development of a VGS provides another opportunity for library and information workers to support research students. Strategically, it is helpful to become involved at the management level of a VGS, e.g. through membership in its steering committee or management group, and to work co-operatively with the team developing and supporting it. This helps to ensure that the library and information perspective is high on the agenda for the VGS.

As illustrated earlier in this chapter, VGSs provide an opportunity for library and information workers to support research students through features such as:

- access to guides and support on using generic and discipline-specific resources
- access to support in developing information literacy and other transferable skills

- named research pathways to guide students through resources to meet the needs of specific disciplines
- mini-video clips and audio recordings with advice and guidance on using library and information resources
- reference services, e.g. via e-mail, SMS messaging or other tools
- current awareness services using RSS, weblogs and other tools.

Summary

This chapter has provided an introduction to the concept of a VGS and presented a detailed case study. The case study illustrated the development of a VGS both as a pilot project in a business school and then across a university. A complementary example followed, highlighting similar points relating to the development of resources, their value to students and the difficulties involved in establishing a virtual community. Engagement with VGS projects provides a further opportunity for library and information workers to work with doctoral students and researchers.

8

Introduction to research communities

Introduction

This chapter considers the importance of research communities in the context of supporting research students. The research process resulting in the publication of new knowledge was described in Chapters 1 and 2. As part of this process, academic researchers may be members of a number of different research communities, including communities based on specific research interests, those that come together around specific activities, e.g. publication of scholarly journals, and online communities. As part of their research development process, doctoral students have the opportunity to join different research communities. This is important because it provides them with access to up-to-date information and ideas, and enables them to network, and it may also have an impact on their future employment.

This chapter covers the following topics: introduction to communities, including communities of practice and communities of interest; research communities; information sharing in research communities; professional associations; academic conferences; online networking; and implications for library and information workers.

What are communities?

> A body of people in the same locality; a group of people who have
> common interests, characteristics or culture.
>
> (*Chambers Dictionary*, 2002)

Membership of one or more research communities, involving either
groups of academics and research students, or groups of academics,
research students, practitioners and other stakeholders, offers
doctoral students an opportunity to come together and share ideas
and experiences, tackle professional and work-based problems and
issues, and engage with their future professional communities.
Research communities are often established to enable like-minded
people or individuals with a common interest to work together and
share ideas or develop new knowledge within a specific subject.
Sometimes communities develop within or across organizations as
the result of a particular organizational structure, e.g. a graduate
school or postgraduate society or research centre. They may also
develop as a result of the need to accelerate research in a particular
subject or because of the interests and enthusiasm of a group of
individuals who want to work together.

Many research communities are characterized by the following:

- a shared interest, e.g. in a particular subject, research approach
  or set of research questions
- shared membership and leadership
- willingness to share ideas and resources
- willingness to provide feedback and support
- autonomous community members
- high levels of dialogue, interaction and collaboration
- information and knowledge sharing
- knowledge construction
- knowledge transfer and knowledge exchange
- use of information and communication technologies.

Communities of practice

The concept of a 'community of practice' has influenced thinking about communities. In their seminal book *Situated Learning*, Jean Lave and Etienne Wenger (1991) adopted the term to describe how professionals learn through collaborative and supportive social interactions. Wenger (2003) defined communities of practice as:

> Groups of people who share a concern, a set of problems, or a passion about a topic, and who deepen their knowledge and expertise in this area by interacting on an ongoing basis. (Wenger, 2003, 4)

At the centre of a community of practice is a group of practitioners who are working together and engaged in developing their practice. For academics this may be their research practice. Lave and Wenger (1991) suggested that knowledge development in professional communities results from social interactions and that individuals who engage with professional communities construct their professional identities in relation to their membership of communities of practitioners. Communities of practice are usually characterized by the following:

- common purpose identified by participants
- shared membership and leadership
- participants likely to be at different stages in their professional lives
- development of professional practice through apprenticeship
- acceptance of low levels of participation by new members, i.e. legitimate peripheral participation
- development, creation and management of knowledge within organizations.
- open ended, not time bound
- importance of dialogue, interaction and shared narratives.

This is relevant to research students, who may have different roles in different communities. In a postgraduate student community they may be active participants and leaders, while within a research community they may be seen as peripheral members who are experiencing a type of apprenticeship as they participate in community activities and develop from students through to becoming core members who are international experts and leaders of the community. Wenger, McDermott and Snyder (2002) identify different levels of participation by individual members within a community of practice, as represented in Figure 8.1. This illustrates three levels: peripheral members, who rarely participate but remain on the sidelines, observing discussions; active members, who join in with discussions when they feel they have something to say; and core members, who introduce new topics or projects and help to shape and lead the community. Wenger, McDermott

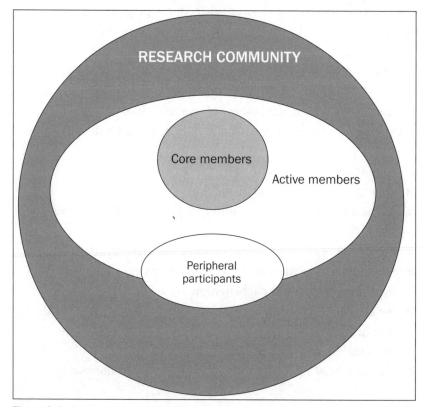

Figure 8.1 *A community of practice*

and Snyder (2002) suggest that there is a development route from peripheral through to active or core membership.

How do research students join a community of practice? For many their starting point is their relationship with their supervisor and their local research community. This may provide them with access to a broader community of practice, perhaps one that spans not only a number of universities but also a number of countries. Research students are likely to gain a range of benefits from their membership in a community of practice. These may be divided into three groups: research-specific, social and career benefits.

Research-specific benefits include:

■ access to information and expertise
■ opportunities for sharing ideas and resources
■ opportunity to obtain feedback on work-in-progress
■ wider perspectives on their discipline.

Social benefits include:

■ access to like-minded individuals
■ support and friendship
■ sense of identity and group membership.

Career benefits include:

■ confidence building
■ development of professional expertise
■ continuing professional development
■ membership of a network.
■ visibility within the research community.

Many communities of practice develop and grow as a result of long-term connections between members, built up through a mixture of working and studying together in different universities, joint activities such as editorship of academic journals and the peer review process, internal and external examining of theses, and other academic activities. These relationships are nurtured through face-to-face meetings, e.g. at conferences and other networking events, through e-mail and other internet-based communications. Joint activities such as developing a collaborative bid for funding, e.g. from a research council, and then working together on a project also help to build communities. Sometimes virtual research communities develop. Some of the benefits of membership in virtual communities of practice are described by Hyams and Mezey (2003, 36), who write:

> virtual communities offer much richer opportunities to share best practice and know-how in an active sense. They can stimulate the sharing of intelligence, and make it possible to harvest, organise and share 'knowledge' for preservation and re-use. They provide common ground for solving problems and sharing insights. . . .Communities offer much more than mere email discussion lists to members, too, because they can share access to resources (including multimedia and datasets), and communicate in real time using facilities such as live chat.

Online communication tools are often used to support interactions within a community of practice, enabling busy researchers and individuals who are geographically isolated from their peers to access a community of peers at a time and place that suits them. Virtual communities of practice may be mediated in a number of different ways:

- via a virtual learning environment such as Blackboard or WebCT[1]
- using collaborative communications software such as iCohere[2]
- via a website providing access to communications tools such as discussion groups and chat software

■ using Web 2.0 tools such as weblogs, wikis or social networking software such as Facebook™, MySpace™ or LinkedIn™.

Communities of interest

Alongside the idea of a community of practice is the concept of a 'community of interest'. These are large groups or networks, perhaps involving hundreds of people, and they support the dissemination and exchange of information. Communities of interest develop when people come together to exchange news or information about a specific topic. For research students this may include membership of an e-mail discussion list on a particular aspect of methodology. Table 8.1 is based on the work of Wenger, McDermott and Snyder (2002) and compares learning communities of practice and communities of interest (Allan, 2007).

Table 8.1 *Comparison of communities of practice and communities of interest*		
Characteristics	**Community of practice**	**Community of interest**
Purpose	To problem solve To improve professional practice To improve the effectiveness of an organization or project To create and expand knowledge	To be informed To share ideas and information To meet up with like-minded people
Membership	People who share a particular interest in a topic People who volunteer or are invited to become members Likely to be relatively small, e.g. 6–24 members	People who share a particular interest Likely to be voluntary (self-selected) People who become subscribers or members of a particular group, e.g. e-mail list May be very large, e.g. 12–1000+ members
What holds them together	Interest, commitment, identity with group Personal relationships within the group Some research groups Some research project groups	Access to information and sense of like-mindedness Some open discussion groups supported by professional associations Some e-mail discussion lists

Research communities

All research students have the opportunity to join a number of overlapping research communities when they enrol for their doctoral studies. Some may be communities of interest, e.g. a postgraduate society, and others may be communities of practice, e.g. a research student learning set. This is illustrated in Figure 8.2, which shows an education doctoral student's membership of a number of different communities.

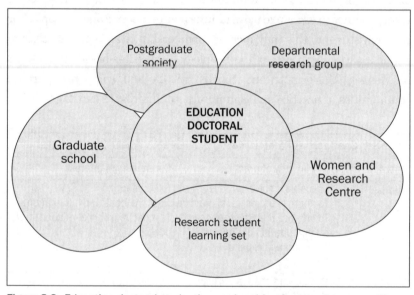

Figure 8.2 *Education doctoral student's membership of research communities within a university*

Figure 8.3 illustrates how a research student's membership of communities may extend beyond the university and encompass both research and professional communities, including alumni networks developed from previous undergraduate or postgraduate studies. Advantages of membership of so many communities is that it offers students opportunities to exchange information and ideas, provides them with access to facilities and resources relevant to their research, and may help them to develop their careers in the future.

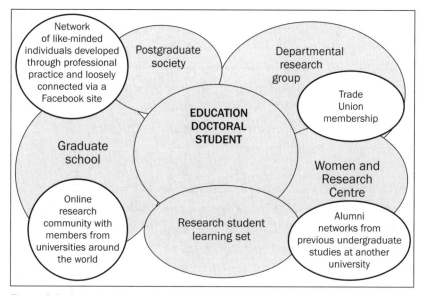

Figure 8.3 *Education doctoral student's membership of research and professional communities*

Information sharing in academic communities

Writing in 1972, Crane developed the concept of invisible colleges or communities of academics and demonstrated their value the most productive members having more social ties, influence and visibility than those who are less productive. There has been extensive research, e.g. Talja (2002), demonstrating the value of such networks or communities in providing experienced academics with access to information sources, and that this is an important means of information acquisition for experienced researchers and academics. Those at an earlier stage in their careers, in contrast, are likely to rely on traditional and comparatively time-consuming information-searching activities, using tools such as databases and citation indexes.

Talja (2002) identified the following types of information-sharing habits within academic communities:

1 Strategic sharing: information sharing as a conscious strategy of maximizing efficiency in a research group.

2 Paradigmatic sharing: information sharing as a means of establishing a novel and distinguishable research approach or area within a discipline or across disciplines.
3 Directive sharing: information sharing between academics and students.
4 Social sharing: information sharing as a relationship- and community-building activity.

This work is relevant to research students and their development for a number of reasons. First, they may be involved in two types of information-sharing activity, i.e. they may be recipients of directive information sharing in the early stages of their research when they receive information and advice from their supervisors. Second, they may be involved in information sharing as both a relationship-building and a community-building activity with other research students and with academics.

Talja (2002) also identified the following types of sharing processes that may occur:

■ Super-sharing takes place in longitudinal closely knit research projects in which information sharing has been adopted as a conscious productive strategy. All types of information sharing take place in such projects.
■ Sharers work together in temporary writing projects or research groups combined with an interest in making sense of or establishing a novel research problem, approach, or area. All types of information sharing take place in such groups.
■ Occasional sharing takes place between colleagues who do not share the same research interest or subject, or between teachers and students. The forms of sharing are mainly limited to sharing information about relevant documents and about ways of finding relevant documents. Documents and information about the contents of relevant documents are less often shared.
■ Non-sharing is combined with research projects that are unique

in the sense that no one else either in the immediate work community or in virtual research communities shares the same research interest or subject.

These different forms of information sharing are of interest, because in order to engage with this type of community activity an individual needs something to share, e.g. data, information or documents. New doctoral students or early-career researchers may be limited in what they are able to share within a research community, though they will always be able to share their ideas and apply their critical thinking to current issues.

Professional associations

People working within a particular profession, e.g. accountancy, economics, human resource management, nursing, medicine or social work, keep in touch with each other by becoming involved in local, regional, national or international networks. Many such networks are established and maintained by professional associations such as the Chartered Institute for Personnel and Development (CIPD) the Chartered Management Institute (CMI) or the British Medical Association (BMA).

Professional associations are relevant to research students for a number of reasons. First, they often provide reduced-rate student membership which brings with it a range of benefits, including access to library and information resources, to professional and sometimes academic journals and to networks and other groups. Second, for some researchers, the professional association may become a source of data or information for their research. For some research students, professional associations are also important to their long-term careers because they provide a means of becoming a chartered practitioner, the association providing access to professional development and quality assurance for new members of the profession.

Some professional associations have their own library and information service and will provide detailed advice and guidance by phone or by e-mail. This may be useful to research students doing professional doctorates who need certain types of information, e.g. policy documents relating to practice. Professional associations may also provide support, advice, training and development via workshops and other training events. These are generally offered at the association's headquarters and at venues around the country. In addition, many local and specialist groups offer training events and these are frequently relatively cheap to attend and don't involve high travel costs. Professional conferences are also a good way for research students to take part in practitioner networks, and often offer reduced rates for students.

Many professional activities occur through online communication tools such as discussion groups and mailing lists. Discussion groups can be used in a variety of ways and, in general, they provide forums for:

- requests for factual information
- requests for advice and opinions or experiences
- information about new websites, products, publications
- advice on buying or using new systems or products
- conference and meeting announcements
- staff development announcements
- information about vacancies, some of which will not be published in the open press or via other means.

There are thousands of academic research groups and professional associations. A few will be mentioned here to illustrate the typical activities of this type of organization.

The Royal Economic Society (RES) on its website at www.res.org.uk, describes itself as 'a professional association promoting the encouragement of the study of economic science in academic life, government service, banking, industry and public affairs'. It provides an extensive range of benefits for members, including student members, such as publications, library, conferences and other events, discussion boards, etc. It organizes an annual PhD presentation meeting, the aim of which is 'to provide a service both for UK economics university departments and other European economics departments wishing to recruit lecturers, and for PhD students seeking academic jobs either in the UK or elsewhere in Europe'. The event is attended by both students and potential employers and is an opportunity to network and to learn about each other's needs. The event involves students making presentations and giving poster sessions, which are used by potential employers to identify new talent for their organizations.

The Royal Society of Chemistry (RSC), on its website at www.rsc.org, describes its worldwide network of more than 46,000 members. The Society provides a vast array of networking opportunities via local sections throughout the UK and the Republic of Ireland, as well as divisions, forums and groups covering a wide range of topics and themes relevant to research, education and development in the chemical industries. It also organizes a range of conferences and events, which offer something for chemists (including research chemists) at different stages in their career. In addition, it has a range of publications (including academic journals) and a library and information centre.

The British Education Research Association (BERA, www.bera.ac.uk) is concerned with educational research. It has a range of special interest groups, and provides them with special online worksites. In addition, BERA offers its members access to conferences, projects and publications as well as links to related associations. As with many societies, it offers special opportunities to research students at its conferences, e.g. poster sessions, so that they can gain confidence and experience in attending and participating in academic conferences.

As many research students become involved in learning and teaching activities, e.g. by leading seminars and working with undergraduates, they also develop the skills required for teaching in a university. In addition to the practice they gain through their teaching activities, they are likely to be students on postgraduate teaching certificate courses. This enables them to become members of new communities with fellow researchers or new academics, whose focus is teaching and learning rather than research, and with the programme teaching team, who may be members of the staff development unit. They may also become involved in the relevant specialist subject group of the Higher Education Academy (HEA). As with other associations, the HEA provides access to conferences and networking activities, publications and resources, as well as opportunities to take part in educational research and development activities.

Academic conferences

Academic conferences are a well established feature of the academic year. They are organized by professional associations, university research centres and units, and special interest groups. Typically, an academic conference involves the following activities:

- keynote addresses where the presenter is invited to speak to the whole conference
- academic paper presentations, selected on the basis of peer review; the papers are often grouped around specific themes and presented in special 'symposia' managed by a chairperson or facilitator
- poster sessions where students, early-career researchers and others may present their initial research findings and ideas
- meetings, e.g. of the organizing committee or groups associated with the sponsoring organization
- exhibitions, e.g. of academic publishers, learned societies
- networking events
- social events, e.g. conference dinner, day or evening excursions.

These are important events because they provide researchers with an opportunity to:

- share and receive feedback on their research findings and ideas
- develop their knowledge by attending the sessions of colleagues
- network with other researchers
- network with publishers of scholarly journals
- socialize.

For student researchers, conferences often provide special sessions to enable them to develop their presentation skills and become involved in poster sessions. Many universities provide financial support to help their research students attend conferences. Some universities provide short courses and workshops on topics such as making a conference presentation, preparing for and making a poster presentation. The following feedback was provided by a PhD student in Gender Studies who attended the 2009 British Association for Management (BAM) annual conference:

> It was wonderful. Very exhausting particularly as it took place during
> Ramadan. I met X whose work I've read. . . . I was disappointed as she
> didn't seem interested in me or my research. I went to a talk by
> Professor Y and she was amazing. Very friendly and helpful. She asked
> me to e-mail her and keep in touch. I went to as many sessions as
> possible and talked to other students – it was interesting comparing
> experiences. We exchanged e-mails and I will keep in touch with them.
> The conference helped me to understand how I fit into the academic
> world. Now, I want to make presentations at different conferences to
> gain experience. I found talking about my work helped me to be
> confident about what I have done. It will help in the viva.

Conferences aimed at research students and early-career researchers are popular. For example, a group called the Northern Advanced Research Training Initiative (NARTI) ran its fifth doctoral colloquium in 2009 and one student wrote about her experience of presenting her research into women leaders in Saudi Arabia:

> I had the privilege of meeting several well known researchers whom I knew from their research papers and even some of the authors of textbooks such as . . . Attending the colloquium was indeed a positive experience. The atmosphere of the colloquium was very friendly, supportive and well organized. It was an excellent opportunity to receive feedback from established experts in the field, and to meet and discuss ideas with those experts. Additionally, meeting other students from different universities and discussing issues that concerned PhD students was extremely helpful. Furthermore, the colloquium gave me an opportunity to network which could be useful for publishing papers or looking for work in the future.

Online networking

Online communication tools and networks have become increasingly important as a means of supporting research communities. A number of these tools were considered in Chapter 7 in the context of virtual graduate schools. This section provides an overview of tools and facilities to support online networking.

There are two main types of online communication process, asynchronous and synchronous. These are described below.

- **Asynchronous tools** enable people to communicate at a time that suits them. Individuals post a message that is held by the system, i.e. communication takes place over time rather than at the same time. This message can be read and responded to as and when the recipient comes online.. Examples include e-mail, discussion boards and weblogs.
- **Synchronous tools** enable people to communicate when they log on to the same system at the same time, i.e. communication is immediate and live. Unlike in face-to-face communications, a

transcript or record of the communication process may be available. Examples of synchronous tools include chat and conference rooms, internet telephony, e.g. Skype™, and video conferencing.

The first generation of virtual communication tools became available during the 1990s and resulted in a range of facilities, including e-mail, e-lists or discussion lists, bulletin boards, online chat and conferencing, and video conferencing. These tools revolutionized teaching, learning and research, and many are available in VLEs and other types of group communications software, which are explored later in this section. They may also be provided on websites owned by bodies such as graduate schools, research centres or professional associations.

A second generation of virtual communication tools, often referred to as social networking software or Web 2.0, has now developed and is used regularly by millions of people. The aim of social networking websites is to provide a space where individuals can meet. As its name suggests, social networking is concerned with individuals making connections with others, using internet-based tools such as weblogs and wikis, and personal sites using facilities such as MySpace™, Facebook™ and LinkedIn™. Some of these tools, e.g. weblogs and wikis, are becoming integrated into virtual graduate schools (see Chapter 7). Millions of people regularly use social networking tools as a way of keeping in touch with friends, making new friends and sharing ideas around the world. For this reason alone, it is important to consider them when identifying approaches to connecting with and supporting research students.

First-generation virtual communication tools

A list of common first-generation virtual communication tools, with their key characteristics, is presented in Table 8.2 (overleaf). Although the tools are presented individually, in practice they are used in combination, e.g. a research community site may use a mixture of chat, discussion boards, e-mail, online questionnaires and video calls.

Table 8.2 *First-generation virtual communication tools (adapted from Allan, 2007)*

	Type of interaction	Asynchronous/ synchronous	E-learning applications
Audio files Bulletin boards, discussion lists or e-lists	One to many One to many	Asynchronous Asynchronous	Exchange audio information Exchange information Detailed instruction Discussions Collaborative or project work Knowledge construction
Chat or conferencing	One to one, one to many	Synchronous	Exchange information Detailed instruction Discussions Collaborative or project work Knowledge construction Networking
E-mail	One to one, one to many	Asynchronous	Exchange information Detailed instruction Knowledge construction Networking
Instant messaging	One to one, one to many	Synchronous	Exchange information Detailed instruction
News digests and news groups	One to many	Asynchronous	Exchange information
Polling and questionnaire software or webforms	One to one, one to many	Asynchronous	Collect information
Video conferencing	One to one, one to a few	Synchronous	Exchange information Detailed instruction Discussions Knowledge construction

Second-generation virtual communication tools

Second-generation or Web 2.0 virtual communication tools include social networking software, communication tools such as Skype™, weblogs, wikis and virtual worlds. These will each be considered in turn.

Social networking tools

Social networking tools are now extensively used for keeping in touch with friends and family. They are also increasingly being used in the context of research activities and it is likely that this use will continue to expand rapidly in coming years. Social networking sites such as Facebook™, MySpace™ and LinkedIn™ enable users to:

- create and design their own site
- personalize their own site, e.g. using photographs and other images
- exchange information and ideas through chat sessions and discussion groups
- exchange files (text, audio, video)
- establish RSS feeds
- post announcements
- send private and group e-mails
- use Twitter™.

Depending on the provider, an individual may restrict access to her website to named contacts, or leave it open to anyone. These sites are extensively used by millions of people and they provide a lively online community. In addition to these general sites there are specialist sites focused on specific topics or themes. For many research students, their social networking site provides an opportunity to engage informally with like-minded people around the world. Observing PhD students in my own department, I am conscious that they often dip into and out of their social networking sites throughout the day, and also constantly receive messages both online and via their mobile phones. Many students appears to be in constant communication with others (even individuals working at the next desk!) using online and other tools. For some students, the boundary between private and academic life is blurred.

Another example of social networking sites is specialist photographic sites such as Flickr™ (www.flickr.com), a site that enables individuals to store, search, sort and share photographs. Bookmarking sites such as Delicious™ (http://delicious.com) provide access to a wide range of websites and networks.

Internet telephony

A commonly used internet communication tool is internet telephony, which integrates internet and telephone functions. A popular system is Skype™ (www.skype.com), which is rather like a regular instant messaging system with free computer-to-computer phone calls between users. It also allows calls to landline and mobile phones anywhere around the world, as well as video calls. You can receive calls to your computer from regular computers, provided that you have a special 'SkypeIn™' subscription.

Weblogs

Weblogs provide a means of personal expression and sharing information via the internet. In some respects, a weblog is rather like an online diary or journal, owned by an individual who uses it to share her experiences. The structure of weblogs varies, but typically they are divided into two or three columns. One column (the central one) normally includes postings or brief paragraphs of opinion, information or personal diary entries, which are arranged chronologically, with the most recent entry first. They may also contain a contents list, a space for visitors to add a comment below a specific entry and other features, e.g. search tool, favourite web links etc. Example weblogs include: Sheila Webber's information literacy blog[3] and and Phil Bradley's weblog.[4] Professional weblogs such as these provide extremely easy access to up-to-date information on specific topics.

Wikis

A wiki is a web page that can be contributed to or edited by any reader. One of the commonest examples of a wiki is Wikipedia, which is described as:

> a multilingual, web-based, free content encyclopedia project. Wikipedia is written collaboratively by volunteers from all around the world. With rare exceptions, its articles can be edited by anyone with access to the Internet, simply by clicking the *edit this page* link. The name Wikipedia is a portmanteau of the words *wiki* (a type of collaborative website) and *encyclopedia*. Since its creation in 2001, Wikipedia has grown rapidly into one of the largest reference Web sites on the Internet. (www.wikipedia.org)

One of the strengths of wikis is that they enable a large number of people to contribute to a set of ideas and develop a resource. The obvious disadvantage is that there is no editorial control over the material, so the quality of the information is variable. Wikis are relevant to researchers because they can be used to host a paper that is being written by a closed group of authors.

Virtual worlds

Some research students become involved in virtual worlds, probably the best known of which is Second Life™, a 3-D virtual world for adults aged 18 and over where one can create an 'avatar' or persona and interact with others in a variety of different settings. These virtual worlds provide different ways in which researchers can meet and work together; they are also sometimes the focus of academic research.

Many of the first- and second-generation communication tools can be brought together in VLEs such as a virtual graduate school or a website hosted by a research centre or professional association. In some respects, this provides a 'one stop' shop for researchers. There are a number of different approaches to providing this type of system:

- subscription-based educational services such as WebCT and Blackboard
- open source systems such as Moodle or Sakai, which offer another approach to developing a VLE
- subscription-based generic services such as iCohere
- group collaboration software such as Lotus Notes, and freely available software such as the group facilities offered by many internet services, e.g. Google groups.

Commonly used social networking sites used by researchers include:

- Academia (www.academia.edu), which provides access to people via their research interests or affiliations as well as news and status updates on members' activities
- The Graduate Junction (www.graduatejunction.com), which supports research students as well as early-career researchers. It describes itself as 'connecting researchers with industry, social enterprise and each other' and provides access to a research network (researchers, groups, conferences), resources (writing across boundaries, posters support, graduate journals, published literature and taking a break), blogs and advice forum.
- sites such as Find a PHD, Vitae and Find a Professional Doctorate.[5]

Many academic journals provide blogs to help support and encourage authors and aspiring authors. A good example from the journal *Nature* is Nautilis.[6] This blog provides an extensive range of entries, is kept up to date and provides information about different types of opportunity that are relevant to researchers. In addition, *Nature* supports a blog that is concerned with peer reviewing[7] and which provides valuable guidance on current and future peer reviews. Postings on this blog would also be of interest to authors and aspiring authors, as they provide an inside view of the peer review process.

Implications for library and information workers

Part of the doctoral process involves students in joining and becoming active members of communities of practice and in engaging with broader communities of interest. This is an important part of their development and also appears to be very important in terms of their entry into academic research careers. How can the library or information worker facilitate this process?

It would be difficult for an individual or a team of library and information workers to provide current information on all of the relevant research groups and communities, professional associations, conferences and different forms of social networking. However, it is important to be able to provide information and guidance to students so that they can appreciate the benefits of becoming involved in these professional activities. In the case of liaison and research librarians who work within a particular discipline or provide support for specific research teams, it is possible to provide more focused and detailed information and advice.

My own experience is that once research students become aware of the range of communities and networking opportunities that are open to them, they often become extremely enthusiastic about joining them. In particular, as they approach the final stages of writing their theses and start thinking about their *viva* examinations and life beyond, the importance of engaging with professional networks becomes apparent. Many universities, graduate schools, faculties and departments are willing to provide funding to support these research student activities.

Summary

This chapter has provided an outline description of research communities, including a discussion about communities of practice and communities of interest. A number of different forms of academic community have been explored, including professional associations, conferences and online communities. Becoming involved in different professional communities provides research students with access to ideas, information and feedback as well as a social network. It also provides them with opportunities to become visible and to develop their networks and career contacts.

Notes

1 Blackboard and WebCT are both available from www.webct.com.
2 www.iCohere.com.
3 http://information-literacy.blogspot.com.
4 www.philbradley.typepad.com.
5 www.findaphd.com/students/life.asp; www.vitae.ac.uk/; and www.professionaldoctorates.com/.
6 http://blogs.nature.com/nautilis.
7 http://blogs.nature.com/peer-to-peer/.

9
Professional development

Introduction

In this chapter I consider different approaches to professional development for library and information workers who are supporting research students. These include support offered by professional organizations and networks, provision offered by higher education institutions, and research degrees. The chapter ends with conclusions relating to the book as a whole.

In Chapter 1, I noted that although the library and information profession is a graduate one there are relatively few practitioners who have obtained a research degree. This means that most LIS practitioners will not have experienced and internalized the processes involved in gaining a doctorate. However, many will have experience of undertaking research activities, e.g. a dissertation as part of an undergraduate or postgraduate degree, or an investigative project as part of normal professional activities. What are the differences between an investigative workplace project and academic research of the type done by doctoral students? Some authors, e.g. Cohen, Manion and Morrison (2000), summarize the differences between academic research and investigative work-based activities, which they label 'evaluation'. Some of these differences are outlined in Table 9.1.

Table 9.1 *Differences between research and evaluation*

	Research	Evaluation
Intents and purpose of investigation	Create new knowledge Contribute to theory Make generalizations	Evaluate some aspect of practice Inform future practice
Scope	Varies – from broad to extremely narrow	Often focused on a particular aspect of practice or a particular case study or set of case studies
Origins of study	Individual curiosity Sponsorship from an external organization	Organizational or professional needs Sponsorship from an external organization
Uses of findings	Contribute to knowledge	Contribute to professional practice and decision making
Timeliness	May be open ended, or fixed by external funder	Timescales may be given by employing organization or sponsor
Criteria for judging study	Contribution to knowledge Research methodology Internal and external validity (or equivalent measures for qualitative studies)	Relevance to practice, credibility and trustworthiness
Agenda	May be defined by researcher	May be defined by employing organization or sponsor

However, the distinction between research and evaluation is not as clear cut as is suggested by Table 9.1 and there is overlap between the two concepts. An important distinction between the two is that research is concerned with adding to theory and contributing to academic knowledge, while evaluation is often concerned with judging the quality and impact of an activity or initiative and then using the findings to inform practice, often at a very local level. After reading the foregoing, some readers may identify that they have been involved in evaluation activities, e.g. evaluating student satisfaction with library services, measuring part-time students' use of library and information services or exploring the impact of a new online service for distance-learning students. These types of activity provide a good basis for developing further knowledge about research and the research process.

Professional organizations and networks

A number of organizations provide access to professional development activities relevant to library and information workers who wish to support research students. In the UK these include generic professional associations such as the Chartered Institute of Library and Information Professionals (CILIP), with its specialist groups. Many other professional associations and networks exist, and the following are indicative of the types of organizations that are active in the field in the UK.

ALISS (www.alissnet.org.uk)

ALISS (Association of Librarians and Information Professionals in the Social Sciences) is a not-for-profit unincorporated professional society, formed in April 2005 by the former committee of ASSIGN (Aslib Social Science Information Group and Network). The group provides opportunities for communication and networking amongst social science librarians and also offers development opportunities. ALISS provides news, information, events and resources, and has a number of special interest groups. An example of the support it provides to its members is a set of recommended resources for library induction and information literacy training sessions. These are widely advertised at the start of each academic year.

Library and Information Science Research Coalition (http://lisresearch.org)

The Library and Information Science Research Coalition was established in 2009. Its website states that:

'The broad mission of the LIS Research Coalition is to facilitate a co-ordinated and strategic approach to LIS research across the UK. The Coalition aims to bring together information about LIS research opportunities and results; encourage dialogue between research funders; promote LIS practitioner research and the translation of research outcomes into practice; articulate a strategic approach to LIS research; and promote the development of research capacity in LIS. The Coalition will provide a formal structure to improve access to LIS research, and maximize its relevance and impact in the UK.

The Library and Information Science Research Coalition website is relatively new and at the time of writing is still developing. However, it does provide access to news, events and links, and also has features such as Twitter™.

Research Information Network (www.rin.ac.uk/)

The Research Information Network (RIN) supports the development of effective information strategies and practices for the UK's research community. On its website its states: 'Through conducting research, providing guidance and promoting innovation, we aim to meet the needs of researchers, institutions, funders, information professionals and everyone who plays a role in the research information landscape.'

RIN produces reports on topics relevant to supporting research and researchers. An important example is its report *Mind the Skills Gap: information-handling training for researchers*, which is available on its website. It also organizes events, including seminars and expert workshops. Examples of recent events include:

■ Freedom of information: what's in it for researchers?
■ The changing face of learned and professional societies libraries
■ The data imperative: libraries and research data workshop
■ Research in the open: how mandates work in practice
■ Values and benefits of data sharing and data management

■ What does it cost and who pays? Scholarly communications globally and in the UK.

RIN uses a number of methods to keep in touch with members, including Web 2.0 tools such as Twitter™, Facebook™ and bookmarks in Delicious™. It provides a wide range of online resources and links aimed at supporting library and information workers and including topics such as: publishing resources; funding issues; social networking; libraries of the future; cataloguing, storage and preservation; blogs; useful organizations.

Research Libraries UK (www.rluk.ac.uk)

Research Libraries UK's (RLUK's) vision is that the UK should have the best research library support in the world. Its mission is to work with members and partners, nationally and internationally, to shape and to realize the vision of the modern research library. The association offers a wide range of activities and services, including specialist groups, events and conferences, publications, projects and services, publications and downloads. It offers updating services via RSS feeds.

SCONUL (www.sconul.ac.uk)

The Society of National, College and University Libraries (SCONUL) promotes excellence in library services in higher education and national libraries across the UK and Ireland. On its website SCONUL states: 'All universities in the United Kingdom and Ireland are SCONUL members: so too are many of the UK's colleges of higher education. Also members are the major national libraries both sides of the Irish Sea. Most of our activities are carried out by the heads of library services, often through SCONUL's range of expert groups or our executive Board.' SCONUL provides information on hot topics, e.g. e-learning, human resources, information literacy, performance improvement, scholarly communications and e-research. It has a well established set of publications which often provide useful articles on practices in academic and national libraries.

Membership and involvement in these professional associations and their networks provide library and information workers with a range of development opportunities, which include:

■ short courses and conferences
■ networking
■ publications
■ current awareness services, e.g. via Twitter™ or RSS.

Short courses and workshops are a popular means of professional development and also provide important opportunities for networking. These may be organized by the professional associations or by special interest groups. The following example is of a one-day workshop offered by CILIP.

Example 9.1: One-day workshop – Supporting research students

Aim
The aim of this workshop is to enable library and information workers to improve their support services for research students.

Benefits of attending
By the end of the workshop, participants will be able to:

■ understand the academic research process and the needs of research students
■ identify approaches to supporting research students
■ develop strategies for improving the ways in which they support research students.

Who should attend?

Anyone supporting the academic needs of research students. This includes academic librarians and learning support workers. It also includes individuals involved in providing e-learning support e.g. through a virtual graduate school.

Special notes: This is a practical workshop. Learning and teaching activities involve discussions, case studies and other practical activities.

Indicative programme

- The research process. What is involved in achieving a PhD or other research degrees?
- What do research students expect from academic services?
- How do we communicate with and support research students?
- Designing and delivering training and coaching sessions for research students
- Providing virtual support services: the concept of a virtual graduate school

---

Development offered by higher education institutions

The majority of library and information workers who support research students are working in higher education institutions or their partner bodies. This means that they are working in a culture of education and research where there are many opportunities for professional development. Typical examples include:

- opportunities to carry out research projects
- opportunities to work with research teams
- engagement with the research community
- staff development opportunities.

Research projects

Many UK universities offer all their staff access to funding, e.g. learning innovations funding, Roberts funding, and funding obtained from alumni and other development activities. These funds provide valuable opportunities for accessing resources (including time) for development activities and associated research. Such activities may be located within the library and information service, or they may involve collaboration with colleagues in other departments and faculties. The outputs from these activities may be published within the university or in the professional or research literature. Many such projects may be accepted for publication in the education literature, as well as the library and information academic press, e.g. those with a learning and teaching angle, or in the business, management or marketing literature, for projects related to these fields.

There are often opportunities within a university to carry out research projects. In the UK they may be funded by external bodies such as JISC (the Joint Information Services Committee), whose website at www.jisc.ac.uk provides examples of its projects, including some major research projects. Organizations such as JISC regularly put out calls for tender and provide valuable opportunities for undertaking important development and research activities.

Working with research teams

In my own career, as an inexperienced researcher I worked to become a member of an experienced research team, and working with this team helped me to develop my confidence and skills. As a result of my membership in a number of teams I was then able to start instigating bids and research activities. This process, which took a number of years, provided me with insight into the bidding process, project management, report writing and producing and publishing academic research. In general, I found colleagues were willing to include me in their teams, and in the initial stages my enthusiasm and willingness to work collaboratively, as well as my skills set, were welcome.

Engagement with the research community

Many library and information workers develop their knowledge of research and skills in supporting research students through their involvement in the research life of the university. This may include active membership of research committees (at university, faculty or departmental levels) and of relevant staff/student committees, or involvement in the activities of the graduate school (or equivalent body). It may include working in a specialist way to support individual research centres or groups, e.g. in the preparation of bids, or documents such as those required in the 2008 UK higher education Research Assessment Exercise (RAE) and in the forthcoming Research Excellence Framework (REF) exercise, provision of specialist information services, and writing literature reviews, reports and academic articles. Attendance at specialist seminars and inaugural lectures are useful ways of learning more about research and research activities.

Staff development opportunities

A wide range of staff development opportunities exist within universities and their partner institutions. Typical examples include:

- short-course programmes offered by a central staff development unit
- training courses and modules offered by a graduate school (or its equivalent)
- e-learning and blended learning training opportunities
- workshops and conferences offered by departments and faculties.

Research degrees

Another approach to professional development is to undertake a research degree on a full- or part-time basis. The range of research degrees was explored in Chapter 1. Library and information workers can to find details of the types of research degree offered by library and information departments in universities by visiting their websites (in the UK, CILIP[1] provides a list of these educational providers). A typical example from the UK is that of the Department of Information Studies at the University of Aberystwyth in Wales, which offers both MPhil and PhD programmes in librarianship and in information science. Another example is the Robert Gordon University in Aberdeen, Scotland, which offers full-time and part-time MPhil and PhD programmes. It also offers professional doctorates, either DBA (Doctor in Business Administration) or DInfSci (Doctor in Information Science), which enable practitioners to do research that is linked to real-world issues.

In addition to research degrees in the field of library and information sciences, it is possible to study for a doctorate in a related field. For example, I built on MA and MEd studies in the field of education by completing a Doctorate in Education, which enabled me to explore my interest in e-learning and e-mentoring. A colleague who was a manager in an academic library developed her career by completing first an MBA and then a DBA in the field of management. Information in Chapters 1 and 3 provides guidance on finding out more about research degrees.

Conclusion

In this book I have explored different aspects of supporting research students. My starting point in Chapters 1 and 2 was researchers and research processes. This was followed by a description of the typical learning, development and research processes experienced by doctoral students in Chapters 3 and 4. I then considered the skills required by doctoral students and discussed them, in Chapter 5, in the context of initiatives in the UK to improve not only research skills but also the employability of people with doctorates.

In Chapter 6, I considered different approaches to supporting research students, including induction, workshops, one-to-one support and electronic support. This was followed by a discussion about different approaches for targeting and communicating with research students. An increasingly important means of supporting research students is through a virtual graduate school and this concept was explored in some depth in Chapter 7 and illustrated with case studies. Virtual graduate schools often support communities of researchers. Research communities are important because they support knowledge creation and exchange, scholarly publishing, and the development of networks. Two different types of community, communities of practice and communities of interest, were explored in Chapter 8 in the context of their relevance to research students. Membership in a research community is important for research students because it helps to provide them with access to information, ideas, networking and career support. Library and information workers who are knowledgeable about such communities and networks can signpost students towards them.

Finally, in this chapter I have considered different approaches to professional development for library and information workers. These include support offered by professional organizations and networks, provision by higher education institutions and research degrees.

Supporting research students is currently high on the agenda of universities in the UK. Research skills training for research students is seen as vital to successful completion of their degrees, as well as having an impact on their employment prospects. Developing strategic and targeted support for these students is an important element in the role of library and information workers.

Current research students are the academics of the future and our activities in supporting them will have a long-term impact. I hope that this book will contribute to work in this area and that library and information workers – who are possibly juggling with heavy workloads and competing demands – will be able to use it to help them support research students.

Notes

1 www.cilip.org.uk.

References and bibliography

References

Allan, B. (2007) *Blended Learning*, Facet Publishing.

Banks, S., Wellington, J. and Joyes, G. (2008) Professional Doctorates and Emerging Online Pedagogies. In *Proceedings of the 6th International Conference on Networked Learning, 5 and 6 May 2008, Halkidiki, Greece*, 9–15.

Barry, C. A. (1997) Information Skills for an Electronic World: training doctoral research students, *Journal of Information Science*, **23** (3), 225–38.

Bell, J. (1999) *Doing your Research Project. A guide for first-time researchers in education and social science*, Open University.

Bryman, A. and Bell, E. (2007) *Business Research Methods*, Oxford: Oxford University Press.

Chambers Dictionary (2002) *Chambers 21st Century Dictionary*, Chambers.

Chiang, K. H. (2003) Learning Experiences of Doctoral Students in UK Universities, *International Journal of Sociology and Social Policy*, **23** (1/2), 4–32.

Chu, S. K. W. and Law, N. (2006) Development of Information Search Expertise: research students' knowledge of source types, *Journal of Librarianship and Information Science*, **39** (1), 27–40.

Cohen, L., Manion, L. and Morrison, K. (2000) *Research Methods in Education*, 5th edition, Routledge/Falmer.

Crane, D. (1972) *Invisible Colleges: diffusion of knowledge in scientific communities*, University of Chicago Press.

Elbow, P. (1973) *Writing Without Teachers*, Oxford University Press.

Hyams, E.and Mezey, M. (2003) Virtuous Virtual Weblogs: the new internet community?, *Library and Information Update*, **2**, 36–7.

Lave, J. and Wenger, E. (1991) *Situated Learning: legitimate peripheral participation*, Cambridge University Press.

Loureiro-Koechlin, C. (2008) *Evaluation of the Virtual Graduate School*, Hull University Business School.

Park, C. (2007) *Redefining the Doctorate*, Higher Education Academy, www.hea.ac.uk.

Phillips, E. M. and Pugh, D. S. (2000) *How to Get a PhD*, 3rd edition, Open University Press.

Radnor, H. A. (2001) *Researching Your Professional Practice: doing interpretive research*, Open University

RIN (2008) *Mind the Skills Gap: information-handling training for researchers*, www.rin.ac.uk.

Roberts Review (2002) *Set for Success: the supply of people with science, engineering and technology skills*, UK Department of Trade and Industry and Department of Education and Skills.

SCONUL (Society of College, National and University Libraries) (2006) *The Seven Pillars of Information Literacy*, www.sconul.ac.uk/groups/information_literacy/sp/seven_pillars.html.

Sikes, P. and Goodson, I. (2003) Living Research: thoughts on educational research as moral practice. In Sikes P. et al. (eds) *The Moral Foundation of Educational Research: knowledge, inquiry and values*, Milton Keynes: Open University Press.

Stauffer, T. M. (1990) A University Model for the 1990s, *New Directions for Higher Education*, **18** (2), 19–24.

Talja, S. (2002) *Information Sharing in Academic Communities: types and levels of collaboration in information seeking and use*, www.uta.fi/~lisaka/Taljaisic2002_konv.pdf.

UK Research Councils (2001) *Joint Statement of the Research Councils'/AHRB's [Arts and Humanities Research Board's] Skills Training Requirements for Research Students,* www.qaa.ac.uk/academicinfrastructure/codeOfPractice/.

Webb, J., Gannon-Leary, P. and Bent, M. (2007) *Providing Effective Library Services for Research,* Facet Publishing.

Wellington, J. (2000) *Educational Research: contemporary issues and practical approaches,* Continuum.

Wellington, J., Bathmaker, A. M., Hunt, C., McCulloch, G. and Sikes, P. (2005) *Succeeding with Your Doctorate,* Sage.

Wenger, E., McDermott, R. and Snyder, W. M. (2002) *Cultivating Communities of Practice,* Harvard Business School.

Wenger, E. (2003) *Communities of Practice: learning, meaning and identity,* Cambridge University Press.

Wisker, G. (2001) *The Postgraduate Student Handbook,* Palgrave.

Bibliography

Austin, A. E. (2002) Preparing the Next Generation of Faculty: graduate school as socialization to the academic career, *The Journal of Higher Education,* **73** (1), 94–122.

Banks, S., Wellington, J. and Joyes, G. (2008) Professional Doctorates and Emerging Online Pedagogies. In *Proceedings of the 6th International Conference on Networked Learning, 5 and 6 May 2008, Halkidiki, Greece,* 9–15.

Barjak, F. (2006) Role of the Internet in Informal Scholarly Communications, *Journal of the American Society for Information Science,* **57** (10), 1350–67.

Barnacle, R. (2005) Research Education Ontologies, *Higher Education Research and Development,* **24** (2), 179–88.

Barrett, E. (2003) *Spirit, Trust, Interaction and Learning: a case study of an online community of doctoral students,* paper given at British Educational Research Association Conference, Edinburgh, www.leeds.ac.uk/educol/documents/0003184.htm.

Barry, C. A. (1997) Information Skills for an Electronic World: training doctoral research students, *Journal of Information Science*, **23** (3), 225–38.

Bawden, D. (2001) Information and Digital Literacies: a review of concepts, *Journal of Documentation*, **57**, 218–59.

Bell, A. (1997) The Impact of Electronic Information on the Academic Research Community, *New Review of Academic Librarianship*, **3**, 1–24.

Bradford, C. (2005) University of Warwick: impact of the library on the research process, *Library and Information Research*, **29** (1), 52–4.

Buschman, J. and Warner, D. A. (2005) Researching and Shaping Information Literacy Initiatives in Relation to the Web: some framework problems and needs, *Journal of Academic Librarianship*, **31**, 12–18.

Chiang, K. H. (2003) Learning Experiences of Doctoral Students in UK Universities, *International Journal of Sociology and Social Policy*, **23** (1/2), 4–32.

Chu, S. K. W. and Law, N. (2007) Development of Information Search Expertise: research students' knowledge of source types, *Journal of Librarianship and Information Science*, **39**, 27–40.

Collinson, J. A. (2005) Artistry and Analysis: student experiences of UK practice-based doctorates in art and design, *International Journal of Qualitative Studies in Education*, **8** (6), 713–28.

Cox, A. (2005) What are Communities of Practice? A comparative review of four seminal works, *Journal of Information Science*, **31** (6), 527–40.

Deem, R. and Brehony, K. J. (2000) Doctoral Students' Access to Research Cultures: are some more unequal than others? *Studies in Higher Education*, **25** (2), 149–65.

East, J. W. (2005) Information Literacy for the Humanities Researcher: a syllabus based on information habits research, *Journal of Academic Librarianship*, **31** (2), 134–42.

Elkins, J. (2004) Theoretical Remarks on Combined Creative and

Scholarly PhD Degrees in the Visual Arts, *Journal of Aesthetic Education*, **38** (4), 22–31.

Enders, J. (2005) Border Crossings: research training, knowledge dissemination and the transformation of academic work, *Higher Education*, **49**, 119–33.

Espionoza-Ramos, R. and Hammond, M. (2008) Can ICT Build a Solid Bridge to a More 'Engaged' and Collaborative Practice in Doctoral Study?: paradoxes, constraints and opportunities. In *6th International Conference on Networked Learning 5 and 6 May 2008, Halkidiki, Greece*, 112–18.

Gomersall, A. (2007) Literature Searching: waste of time or essential skill?, *Evidence and Policy*, **3** (2), 301–20.

Green, H. and Powell, S. (2005) *Doctoral Study in Contemporary Higher Education*, Open University Press.

Harrison, M. K. and Hughes, F. (2001) Supporting Researchers' Information Needs: the experience of the Manchester Metropolitan University Library, *New Review of Academic Librarianship*, **7**, 67–86.

Johnson, D. (2005) Assessment Matters: some issues concerning the supervision and assessment of work-based doctorates, *Innovations in Education and Teaching International*, **42** (1), 87–92.

Joyes, G. and Banks, S. (2008) Using Technology in Research Methods Teaching. In Donnelly, R. and Mcsweeney, F. (eds), *Applied E-Learning and E-Teaching in Higher Education*, Idea Group Inc, 220–41.

Kammler, B. (2008) Rethinking Doctoral Publication Practices: writing from and beyond the thesis, *Studies in Higher Education*, **33** (3), 283–94.

Lave, J. and Wenger, E. (1991) *Situated Learning: legitimate peripheral participation*, Cambridge University Press.

Lee, A. (2008) How are Doctoral Students Supervised? *Studies in Higher Education*, **33** (3), 267–82.

Lee, A. and Green, B. (2009) Supervision as Metaphor, *Studies in*

Higher Education, **34** (6), 615–30.

Leonard, D. and Metcalfe, J. (2006) *Review of Literature on the Impact of Working Context and Support on the Postgraduate Research Student Learning Experience*, Higher Education Academy.

Leonard, D., Becker, R. and Coate, K. (2005) To Prove Myself at the Highest Level: the benefits of doctoral study, *Higher Education Research and Development*, **24** (2), 135–49.

Lester, S. (2004) Conceptualising the Practitioner Doctorate, *Studies in Higher Education*, **29** (6), 757–70.

MacKenzie, A. and Breen, E. (2008) Information Strategies for Researchers: where are we making a difference? Presented at *SCONUL Working Group on Information Literacy/SCONUL Advisory Group on Information Literacy event, 31 January, Dublin City University*, conference report, *SCONUL Focus*, **43** (Spring), 87.

Malfroy, J. (2005) Doctoral Supervision, Workplace Research and Changing Pedagogic Practices, *Higher Education Research and Development*, **24** (2),165–78.

Mason, R. and Rennie, F. (2007) Using Web 2.0 for Learning in the Community, *The Internet and Higher Education*, 10 (3), 196–203.

McAlpine, L., Jazvac-Martek, M. and Hopwood, N. (2007) Doctoral Student Experience: events that contribute to feeling like an academic/belonging to an academic community. In *SRHE Conference Proceedings 2007, 11–13 December, Brighton, Sussex*, Society for Research into Higher Education, www.srhe.ac.uk/conference2007/.

Mullins, G. and Kiley, M. (2002) It's a PhD, not a Nobel Prize: how experienced examiners assess research theses, *Studies in Higher Education*, **27** (4), 369–86.

Park, C. (2005) New Variant PhD: the changing nature of the doctorate in the UK, *Journal of Higher Education Policy and Management*, **27** (2), 189–207.

Park, C. (2007) *Redefining the Doctorate*, Higher Education

Academy, www.hea.ac.uk.

Phillips, E. M. and Pugh, D. S. (2000) *How to get a PhD: a handbook for students and their supervisors*, Open University Press.

Pinfield, S. (1998) The Use of BIDS ISI in a Research University: a case study of the University of Birmingham, *Program-Electronic Library and Information Systems*, **32**, 225–40.

Powell, S. and Green, G. (eds) (2007) *The Doctorate Worldwide*, Society for Research into Higher Education (SRHE), Oxford University Press.

RIN (2006) *Researchers and Discovery Services: behaviour, perceptions and needs*, www.rin.ac.uk.

RIN (2008) *Mind the Skills Gap: information-handling training for researchers*, www.rin.ac.uk.

Roberts Review (2002) *Set for Success: the supply of people with science, engineering and technology skills*, UK Department of Trade and Industry and Department of Education and Skills.

Sarros, J. C., Willis, R. J. and Palmer, G. (2005) The Nature and Purpose of the DBA: a Case for Clarity and Quality Control, *Education and Training*, 47 (1), 40–52.

Scott, D., Brown, A., Lunt, I. and Thorne, L. (2004) *Professional Doctorates: integrating professional and academic knowledge*, Oxford: Oxford University Press.

Talja, S. (2002) *Information Sharing in Academic Communities: types and levels of collaboration in information seeking and use.* Available at: www.uta.fi/~lisaka/Taljaisic2002_konv.pdf.

Tsai, M. J. and Tsai, C. C. (2003) Information Searching Strategies in Web-based Science Learning: the role of internet self-efficacy, *Innovations in Education and Teaching International*, 40, 43–50.

UK GRAD (2006) *Evaluation of Skills Development of Early Career Researchers: a strategy paper from the Rugby Team*, www.vitae.ac.uk/.

UK GRAD (2006) *A Survey into Career Motivations and Expectations of Doctoral Researchers*, www.vitae.ac.uk/.

Vibert, N., Rouet, J. F., Ros, C., Ramond, M. and Deshoullieres, B. (2007) The Use of Online Electronic Information Resources in Scientific Research: the case of neuroscience, *Library and Information Science Research*, **29**, 508–32.

Wellington, J. and Sikes, P. (2006) A Doctorate in a Tight Compartment: why do students choose a professional doctorate and what impact does it have on their personal and professional lives? *Studies in Higher Education*, **31**, 723–34.

Wellington, J., Bathmaker, A. M., Hunt, C., McCulloch, G. and Sikes, P. (2005) *Succeeding with Your Doctorate*, Sage .

Wikeley, F. and Muschamp, Y. (2004) Pedagogical Implications of Working with Doctoral Students at a Distance, *Distance Education*, **25** (1), 125–43.

Wisker, G. (2001) *The Postgraduate Student Handbook*, Palgrave.

Wisker, G., Robinson, G., Trafford, V., Lilly, J. and Warnes, M. (2004) Achieving a Doctorate: metalearning and research development programmes supporting success for international distance students, *Innovations in Education and Teaching International*, **41** (4), 473–89.

Wood, K. (2006) Changing as a Person: the experience of learning to research in the social sciences, *Higher Education Research and Development*, **25** (1), 53–66.

Wright, T. and Cochrane, R. (2000) Factors Influencing Successful Submission of PhD Theses, *Studies in Higher Education*, **25** (2), 181–95.

Index